LOVE
ADDICTED

One Woman's Spiritual Journey
Through Emotional Dependency

DEBORA M. RICKS

SUNNY HOUSE PRESS

PRINTED IN THE UNITED STATES OF AMERICA

SUNNY HOUSE PRESS
P.O. Box 41592
Baltimore, Maryland 21203-6592

Visit www.DeBoraINK.com
Email: DRICKS6085@aol.com
First Edition published 2005
Library of Congress Control Number 2004116387

ISBN 0-9764031-0-2

*For my baby sister,
my teacher,
LaDawn D. Ricks
and her daughter,
Milan Kane*

CONTENTS

ACKNOWLEDGMENTS

AT LAST, I FULLY APPRECIATE WHAT OTHER AUTHORS MEAN WHEN they say no book is written without the help of many people. More than a few deserve my gratitude—family, friends, and even a foe or two—for contributing to this book in some way. Getting my book to publication has been a long, arduous journey full of sacrifices and struggle, but people who have been willing to graciously extend themselves to me made the journey easier. Sincere thanks to:

God, my Source, for spiritual and emotional healing, courage, and stamina. If any of these four had been lacking, this book would not be.

My dear mother, Mattie S. Hairston Ricks, a queen, for learning to believe in my possibilities and standing as a shining example of self-contentment and love. Mother, I thank you for giving me life. Eyitayo Enitan (Ayo), my sister, friend and one of the most insightful women on the planet, for her unconditional, continual support of my growth and belief in my wildest dreams. Adia, my jewel of a child, for keeping a laugh in my mouth and hope alive in my heart. In Swahili, Adia means, "a gift from God has come." You more than live up to your name. I love and treasure you. Babatunde Enitan Salaam, my inimitable nephew, for your slow smile and brave heart. Young man, you are so destined for greatness!

A special thanks goes to Adrian King, my editor, for his dedication, hard work, and unwavering belief in this work. Your friendship has added immeasurably to the quality of my life. It was your faith in this book that sustained me through times of doubt and difficulty.

Robin Quinn, editor par excellence, for her fiercely keen eye to detail. It was only after Robin's gifted editing that I was finally able to confidently release this work to the world. I take full responsibility for any editing slips you might find.

Tawanda Godwin Huff, for always cheering me on, in word and deed. Harvey B. Wilson, my friend, for spicing things up a bit with the occasional lunch, afternoon movie, and soul nourishing conversations. Wherever you are Harvey, you remain one of my dearest friends. Michael J. Green, for your seamless friendship, unambiguous hugs, and shared laughter. Thanks, Michael, for not letting anything come between us.

Christopher Nwaukwa, for loving me unconditionally. Thanks Chris, for seeing me, listening to me, and hearing me and loving me still. Having you in my life is like money in the bank, even in your absence I feel you backing me up. Eve and Doug Austin, two lovely people with two adorable children, Anna and Ezra, for friendship and opening their hearts and home to Adia and me. Andrew Cary, for blessing me, even as you negotiated an uncertain time in your own life. I hope to return the kindness.

Beverly Spence, for urging me to "Just do it!" when I shared that I wished to write a book. I will be eternally grateful for the kick in the butt. Henry Westray, for offering to open his home to me for a book signing. The planet earth beats with a stronger pulse because you are here. Stan Hines, for never making me have to ask for help and for great talks. You're a good man, Stan.

Michael DeGood, a darling of a man, for setting my life afire and deepening the roots of my resolve to create a life I can love. Your powerful example of a well-lived life continues to reverberate through mine. Margaret "Buffy" Bacon, for an enduring friendship and unwavering support. Love you. Sheila Bennett, for letting me tag along on her business trips to Hawaii and New Orleans. I deeply appreciate your commitment to our many years of friendship.

Bernadette Greene, my eight-grade English teacher, for giving me a concrete foundation, introducing me to Johnny Mathis and, more recently, granting me a second chance. You are a remarkable woman, so easy to love.

Maurice Jackson, for taking good care of "his girls" and our house. We need you still. Chauncey Whitehead, trainer extraordinaire, for standing in the gap for all the brothers who think nothing of letting sisters down. Keep giving sisters what we need—understanding, appreciation and kindness. Sheila "Strawberry" Gaskins, for the camaraderie. Girl, you are so cool! Such a light. Keep shining.

Kenda Bell, a talented powerhouse, for being a friend. I will see you at the top! Nalongo Sayyed, for the radio exposure and, as you say, for being "just a sister away." Teressa Stovall, for badly needed advice delivered with care and grace. Debrena Jackson Gandy, for her generosity of spirit, invaluable advice and encouragement. Patrice Gaines, for helpful feedback.

A special thanks to Cassandra Burton, co-proprietor of Sister Space and Books, Inc., for gently pushing me forward armed with the gift, *The Artist's Way*. Your faith in me helped to get me to this glorious point.

The men whose lives have touched mine, beginning with my father, George G. Ricks. You have shaped, changed, and pushed me into being a better person. I am clear that each of you have come to my door to teach me something about myself. But for you, I would have no stories of love and loss to tell. Bless you all.

All of my sisterfriends, those who are a part of my now and those who once were. I value you all, for each of you has contributed to my becoming.

INTRODUCTION

FOR MANY YEARS I'VE WANTED TO WRITE A BOOK. I BEGAN TO keep a journal in 1985, when my older sister Ayo, to whom I was a bit too emotionally attached, moved to Jamaica with her new lover. I was living in my first apartment, a quaint studio in a brownstone, feeling alone and lonely. I missed my sister, my friend, my confidant. So I bought one of those black and white spotted bound notebooks, picked up a Bic and began a ritual that remains an important spiritual tool to this very day.

Weaving through my copious journal entries, beginning around 1990 is written evidence of my deep longing to write a book. Obviously I was already writing, but my private thoughts, feelings, musings and longings were hardly what I had in mind for a book—at least at that time.

It was in the summer of 1998, as yet another doomed from the start love affair careened to a predictable halt, that I planted myself down in front of my Sony PC and began crafting my story. Not the story you now hold in your hands however. As fate would have it, one day without warning the floppy disk I was using flatly refused me access. After giving in to a fair amount of frustration, reluctantly I surrendered, taking this as a shove from the Universe to move in a different direction. And so I did.

Rather than attempt to rewrite my life story from scratch, I took another approach. Enter my journals. Why endeavor to recreate the wheel, I concluded, when I could make good use of the wheels I'd been spinning for thirteen years via journaling?

This is a book about my messy, protracted journey through love and relationship addiction on a most uneven road toward self-love, wholeness and power. Along with prayer and meditation, journaling has been a vital spiritual ritual. It was and continues to be a process that I engage in religiously. Because my journal writings speak most deeply to my confusion, private sufferings, revelations and joys, they give you a glimpse into the inner workings of the mind of an addict. Thus I've incorporated numerous journal entries—some edited for clarity. Others raw.

However journal entries alone fail. Therefore I provide insight into my youth and early adulthood, and into what I believe to be the genesis of my addiction to men and relationships—a troubled relationship with my father.

As wrong as many of my liaisons seemingly were, I suspected then what I now know—every one of them came to teach me how to better love and honor myself. Hence I add yet another ingredient to the mix, a gathering together of the life lessons that each relationship sought to teach me. This ingredient I've titled *"Gathering My Thoughts."*

Writing a book is no small feat. But, as I have proven, it can be done. I have endured much over the past five or so years to breathe life into this divine assignment. I've abandoned 9 to 5 jobs to make room for the writing life. I've put family matters on hold. And I've made more foolish financial decisions than I care to admit. I guess you might say I chose the difficult path, a road so often traveled by many. But then this truth forms the basis of my book.

All in all, I have few regrets. This was a book that I *had* to pen. Why? Well, for one, God ordained it. That "still small voice" that lives within each of us was unrelenting. It just wouldn't let me be. No matter what I did, who I met, how much (or little) money I had, that voice kept urging me to share my story. Because, as quiet as it is kept in some quarters, love and relationship addiction, i.e. codependency, is a common dis-ease among women, black women included.

Women have been socialized—despite the women's movement, professional and socio-economic progress—to seek completion, fulfillment and wholeness through a man. If you doubt me, notice how often women stay in toxic, abusive relationships rather than being alone. Or consider the number of women who settle for married or otherwise unavailable men only to rationalize their myopic choices with, "*I'd rather have a piece of a man than none at all.*" More significantly, ask yourself why has the rate of HIV/AIDS infection among heterosexual African American women skyrocketed to epidemic proportions? Only unhealthy core beliefs and compulsions could be driving such thinking and behavior. I'm convinced it's an addictive approach to love and relationships rooted in childhood abuse and abandonment, unhealed wounds and self-loathing.

It is my prayer that this book will ignite more candid discourse around this critical but often overlooked issue, especially in the homes, churches, colleges and communities of African Americans. More importantly, I pray that you will find something on these pages that helps you gain greater insight into yourself, heals whatever seeks to keep you bound, and inspires you to move your life forward.

PART ONE

A LOOK BACK

1

ADDICTED TO LOVE

There is no agony like bearing an untold story inside you.
                                        ZORA NEALE HURSTON

*Love is mutually feeding each other, not one living on another
like a ghoul.*

                                                  BESSIE HEAD

I AM AN ADDICT, A RECOVERED ADDICT. FOR MANY YEARS, ONE
stubborn addiction ruled my life. Addiction, as you know, can
take many and varied forms. You've seen them—there are addictions to substances, behaviors, processes and thinking. You
know, perhaps all too intimately, the common compulsions that
can derail the most promising life—alcohol, drugs, sex, work,
overspending, food, gambling—things to which we turn to
avoid ourselves, indulgences we succumb to in an attempt to
numb ourselves against psychic and emotional pain we fear we
can't bear.

Overspending and alcohol have given me pause, yet nothing
has so challenged my life like my addiction to relationships and
men. Yes, I confess, my drugs of choice were love and relationships. An emotional dependent, codependent, whatever you
choose to call a woman determined to siphon identity and
meaning from her "significant" other, I was she. She was I. And
so, a considerable sum of my life's energy has been expended on

finding and keeping a man. This magnificent specimen, so my wounded thinking went, would embody all that I lacked—strength of character, courage in the face of challenge, beauty in mind, body and spirit. In his healing love I'd find wholeness, completion and inner peace. Finally I'd be free. Old fears would go into exile. Faked confidence would become real. That inexhaustible well of toxic shame beneath the façade would be silenced, maybe even disappear. Sweetest deliverances of all, this man would cure the hollowness that throbbed in my belly, that emptiness that neither laudable achievement nor material accumulation was ever able to conquer. Somebody, I prayed, would find me pretty enough, lovable enough, amusing enough, worthy enough to love, protect and provide for. Into womanhood I careened, blindly convinced that the proverbial Mr. Right could fix all that ached within me. With him I'd live blissfully ever after, be safe, protected, and if God were really benevolent I'd also be financially and socially secure. As you might have guessed, with every "failed" relationship, I got closer to this bittersweet truth—nobody or nothing outside me would save me. It would be me, and me alone, who would do it.

ADDICTIONS ARE SYMPTOMS

I say I engaged in relationships addictively since addictions include substances, behaviors and processes that we employ to escape the pain of being people we don't like. Addictions are symptoms of deeper issues that, no matter how much we try, can never cure the illness at the root of the addiction. Addictions are merely convenient escape hatches into which we repeatedly jump to decline life's invitation to grow and evolve. It doesn't matter what your addiction is—food, overspending, alcohol, drugs, sex, relationships, the past—all addictions are enlisted to help us escape from reality, from feelings of inadequacy, insufficiency, hopelessness. Relationships were my drug of choice, the place into which I scuttled in hopes of silencing the resounding inner voice that alone I was not up to the challenges of life.

Addictions are born out of a lack of love, thus it is love and only love that cures them. My father failed to give me the love I needed to feel accepted and whole, so I went in search of it—but in all the wrong places. I might have been addicted to alcohol or food, but that wasn't my path. That may, however, be your path. If it is, you can heal it with love. Self-love. Self-love cures everything. The love you didn't get as a child may have set the stage for the self-loathing and self-sabotaging behaviors you now engage in, but it is self-love that can and will deliver you from continued self-abuse.

Behind addictions, you will find people as afraid of their power and light as they are of their demons. Childhood abuse and abandonment can so impair our sense of self that we will reject our power, beauty and light as fiercely—if not more—as we do our darkness.

Gary Zukav, author of *The Seat of the Soul,* insists that we ought to rejoice when we discover that we have an addiction. I say if you can't get happy about the problem, surely you can celebrate the power within you to heal it. There isn't a trauma, hurt or pain that cannot be healed by love and forgiveness. Besides, nothing hurts us more than holding on to past pain. Own your past, while you work to let go of the pain from it. The journey begins with you embracing your truth.

Here's an indisputable fact—every life is a story. Every story has meaning, because every life story contains treasures, gifts and lessons from which another life might benefit.

This is my story. It is a story of one woman's long and hard journey from emotional bondage to spiritual freedom and self-love.

2

EVERY MAN MY TEACHER

No man is your enemy, no man is your friend, every man is your teacher.

UNKNOWN

Each encounter makes you stronger, even the ones you lose.

MERLE SHAIN, *When Lovers Are Friends*

EVERY PERSON WHO COMES INTO OUR LIFE COMES TO HELP US grow. They come to show us to ourselves, to illuminate the parts of us that we need to see, face, examine and heal. Ignore appearances. Appearances can belie the truth. Everyone, no matter his or her title, apparent role or behavior, is our teacher. Their presence in our life is an invitation to our soul to evolve. Every man I mention here was my teacher, teaching me something about life, its unlimited possibilities, and myself. Thus each man contributed something of great and enduring value to my life. Though all my beloveds presented me with gifts that challenged me to evolve spiritually, sometimes the sweetest gifts enticed me to grow culturally or intellectually. Take Emery, a lover of ancient art and world history with eclectic taste in music that transcends race and culture. Emery taught me to respect my soul's flavor in music, never mind what other people listened to and bought. We'd cruise through Baltimore in his midnight-blue Land Rover, delighting in a potpourri of sounds—new age, blues, country, classical. Once liberated from yet another cultural myth—that black people only like "black music"—my taste in music blossomed. Now on any given day, you might hear a bit of John Lee Hooker and Andrea Bocelli wafting through my open window. Catch me another time and it could be Cesaria Evora and Bonnie Raitt. It all depends on what my soul craves any given moment.

Every man who appeared at my door had a divine hand in shaping my life, pushing it onward, regardless of his—or my own—desires or intentions for the encounter. Every man came bearing gifts, some welcomed, many fiercely resisted. All ultimately changed me for the better. Sometimes my beloved blessed me with one of his profound observations, thus altering the trajectory of my thinking and thus the course of my life. Like the time an otherwise unperceptive lover, on the heels of a heated argument, gently held me in his gaze as he calmly observed, "*Did you know you run whenever you get scared?*" "*Yes, I know,*" I softly admitted. In that moment, my respect and appreciation for this man inched up a notch. Some of my defenses melted away. His seeing me freed me. Honestly, I thought I'd put that tendency behind me, that I'd healed my fear of abandonment. I hadn't. Though I knew this man's days in my life were numbered, his on-point insight deepened my resolve to stop running from my pain so I'd be a better magnet for a better man. But before I stopped running (or at least learned to slow to a trot long enough to consider why I was fleeing), I'd lived life as a serial monogamist. With all that loving and losing came a good deal of heartache and unspeakable pain. And yes, some measure of pleasure. It was, however, the pain that forced me inward, for solace and answers.

FIRST THE PAIN

One guy I was seeing gently clued me in on an idea I'd apparently adopted two years into single motherhood. I believed, he said, that having a baby caused me to lose substantial value as a desirable partner. He was dead right about my thinking. I'd been a childless woman for more than three decades. It was a unique status for a black woman, one I secretly took pride in. I thanked my beloved for his priceless insight, and then made an immediate shift in my self-perception. I loved my child. Though a part of me naturally mourned the loss of my former childless lifestyle, I absolutely wanted my daughter. Being her mother was an honor and a privilege. And my new attitude would decidedly reflect those sentiments. Oh, the power of awareness!

First we experience the pain. Then comes the gain. First we are tested. We pass or we fail. If we pass life's tests, we grow spiritually. If we fail, we are retested. The Universe gives us the same test again though it may appear to be repackaged. When we triumph over adversity, our reward is a testimony. On these pages are my tests and testimonies. I share them with the prayer that my story will give you the courage to look more closely at your own life, at the ways in which you seek for love, peace and power in all the wrong places. If I can finally find love, peace and power, anyone can. If I am able to tap the power within me, so can you. All things are possible, for those who believe in themselves and their possibilities. Dare to believe in you.

3

IN MY FATHER'S HOUSE

Happy or unhappy families are all mysterious.

GLORIA STEINEM

Our first job is to get our own story straight.

NATALIE GOLDBERG

I HAD A PAINFUL CHILDHOOD. THAT'S THE SHORT OF IT. MY father, a charming Pentecostal evangelist and pastor, abused and abandoned me. As a child, there was never a time that I felt loved by him. In fact, I was pretty certain that my father despised me, so intense and ever present was his contempt for me. I was my father's seventh child, my mother's fifth. My parents married after my father's first wife died during childbirth. Into their marriage, my father brought two motherless children, ages five and six. We grew into a big family, eventually there were three boys and six girls. From the childhood stories my senior siblings delight in telling at every family gathering, it's quite clear that my father was a wonderfully loving, gentle and fun parent to them. They evidently had a different father than I did. The father I knew spared neither the rod nor his wrath on me. After decades of trying to piece together plausible reasons for my father's rejection, I have settled the matter with this—my soul was simply on its spiritual path. Fate singled me out to be the repository of this otherwise gentle man's frustrations and fury because from this experience the foundation of my spiritual work was to be put into place. If it's indeed true that we choose our parents before we incarnate, then I chose this father. Why? Well, why not *this* path? *This* was my cross to bear. As far as I have observed, nobody gets through life without experiencing harm, pain and loss—much of which occurs during childhood. The trick is to use your deepest hurt as a stepping-stone toward a life of purpose, passion and power. Truth is, that's precisely what God expects us to do with it.

I'm not sure what it was about *me* that evoked my father's darkness. Maybe something about me mirrored parts of him that he loathed. Perhaps it was the timing of my birth, fourteen months on the heels of my brother Joel's. It could have been the stress and strain of yet another mouth to feed and body to clothe, eleven if you include him and my mother. Or, as was recently suggested by my therapist Rosie, maybe my father's contempt for me was linked to the color of my skin, which was darker than all of his girls up to that point. My caramel colored father, like most of America, was undoubtedly color struck and hence found it impossible to love that which he was trained to hate, even if it was his own flesh and blood. In any event, if don Miguel Ruiz, author of *The Four Agreements*, is correct, how my father treated me had nothing to do with me. I'm not to take it personally. It was all about my father, about how he felt about himself and his life. My father was busy working out his own soul's salvation. I, his unsuspecting little girl, merely had a small part in *his* movie.

A quiet, observant child, I felt as if I lived on the periphery of my family's life, watched and yearned. My mother's time didn't belong to us, at least not directly, but to her unapologetic cycle of chores—cooking, cleaning, washing, ironing, cooking, cleaning, washing, ironing–around the clock! Since she didn't have the luxury of being a "kept" wife, mother cleaned the homes of white people so as to contribute to my father's income from his blue-collar jobs and evangelism. A proud, stoic woman, mother wasn't one to lament her lot. She completely gave herself over to her roles. I never begrudged my mother for not engaging us emotionally, until much later after I'd sufficiently dissected my difficult childhood and her role in it. I've now come full circle. Today I recognize my mother as the queen that she is. Besides, work, work, work and no play was just the way life was lived back then. Such quiet devotion to one's family equaled love. And still, as the mother of a bright, loquacious ten-year-old I consider those childhood times missed opportunities for parent-child communion. But I never questioned my mother's love for me. Her love for her children was—and remains—as solid and steady as the Rock of Gibraltar. I had my mother; it was a loving connection with my father that life cheated me out of.

YOU WILL NEVER AMOUNT TO ANYTHING

While my father pampered and praised, coddled and adored my five sisters, I was belittled, berated, ignored and beaten. Yet no beating cut as deep as the venomous battery of words he'd daily hurl at my self-esteem—*You're just lazy! You look just like a jezebel! You got too much pride! Who do you think you are!* Thankfully, I have forgotten many of the insults. There was one verbal assault, however, that owned me. It seeped into my subconscious mind, then rippled wildly through my life producing bad and—surprisingly—some good fruit. "*You'll never amount to anything,*" he raged. His words tore at my sense of self, forcing me, unconsciously, to labor for years to prove him wrong. Man has yet to construct the belt that can lacerate human flesh like harsh words can hack away at a child's self-esteem. My father's whippings were enraged, out-of-control displays of hate, but few. Time healed my open flesh. My psychic wounds have required considerably more to mend. They've demanded time *plus* spiritual healing work—like fumbling in the dark, falling on my face, pulling myself up, finding my way, losing myself, grieving my losses, practicing forgiveness, crying over what could have been, and trying to love myself through it all.

When I was fourteen, my father ceased to give me money for transportation to school and lunch. "*You're too proud,*" he'd bark. "*When you learn to say 'please' and 'thank you' I'll give you money for school!*" I flat out refused to grovel for what he gave my sisters generously. Besides, wasn't being provided for my birthright? I let him be right. I would be too proud to beg. What my father meant for harm only operated to make me stronger, more determined to go to school, more committed to succeeding despite the obstacles. I would make it with or without him, my teenage mind decided. "And one day," I promised myself, "I won't need you!"

I pined for my father's love, well into womanhood. I couldn't help it. I needed him. In the African American community, there has been quite a bit of misguided dialogue around the importance of an involved father to a boy's healthy development. A boy's chances of maturing into a self-assured, productive man, so the discourse goes, dramatically dwindle when he's denied a relationship with his father. Absolutely. This is right on point. Then there's a growing cadre of shortsighted sisters who insist that their child, boy or girl, "don't need NO father!" These rejected fathers, I might note, are the same men these women felt compelled to bed. This myopia flies in the face of God and common sense. As I see it, if two parties must join together to *create* a life, then wouldn't it follow that both people are essential to the *development* of this life? Attempting to dispense with or marginalize one half of this equation—most often the father—dishonors our children, God and us. Personally, I know men (and women) who have grown into adulthood secretly hungering for their absent or abusive fathers. Those not on the road to emotional healing can be so burdened by shame, bitterness and fear that they are emotionally unfit for the delights and demands of intimate love. Convinced that they are intrinsically flawed, intimacy shines too bright a light on their real selves for them to fully participate in a loving partnership. So they hide, evade and run from love, even as they hopelessly yearn for it.

A GIRL NEEDS A FATHER

A loving, involved father is essential to every child's emotional and spiritual well-being. A father's unconditional love helps to anchor a girl's life while it lays the foundation upon which she can build healthy, balanced expectations for future relationships with men. Moreover, a father's love diminishes the likelihood that a growing girl will attempt to satisfy her need for male adoration and attention by engaging in risky, promiscuous sexual behavior. A father's love is indispensable. Please don't discount it.

My father failed to love me. Consequently I struggled mightily to love myself. My severely compromised self-esteem functioned as a potent magnet for unhealed men, men who unwittingly wrestled with their own ghosts from the past. Meeting men was not the problem, keeping a relationship afloat was. I'd meet men anywhere and everywhere—at work, at school, on the street, in the store, on the bus. As fast as these men came, they left. It confused me. I'd adorn myself with due care, but behind the fastidious clothes and meticulously coiffed hair lurked a woman who thought she was damaged, unwanted goods. It was my needy, wounded girl self who created my circumstances not the woman I wanted the world to think I was.

When I was in my twenties, Sam was my fiercely protective older guy friend in whom I confided all my boyfriend drama. After suffering through yet another one of my episodes he gingerly offered what he believed to be an answer to my love hunger. "Dee," Sam whispered as he leaned in close to me. "Instead of always looking for someone to love *you*. Pause. "Why don't you try *loving*?" Huh? Do *what*? What was he talking about? Sam's pearls of wisdom, though utterly impossible for me to then execute, are forever etched in my mind because I intuitively knew they held profound significance.

Sam, however, failed to appreciate just how emotionally wounded I was. I had no love *inside* me to give anybody, not even me. Besides, love was something a woman got, not gave. If and when it was ever offered. At least, that's what I learned from observing my parents. Yes, men gave love and women received—or rejected—it.

Our core beliefs, not the occasional thought, inspire our choices and decisions. Some part of me desired true love. Another part of me feared it. Thus my anxiety peaked whenever love drew near. So as to escape the pain of happiness, I'd sabotage love. Or I'd keep happiness at bay, always pining for love but never allowing it in. I had a knack for attracting all the wrong men, unavailable men on whom there were prior claims—claims made by other women, alcohol, drugs, work, a jealous past. Men who desired me bored me. Once in a relationship, whenever the love boat sailed into calm waters, happiness anxiety managed to steer it right into the eye of a raging storm. You might say the certainty that I was unworthy of love set the stage for the off Broadway dramas and tragedies–and comedies—that I called love.

Children who do not feel loved enter adulthood emotionally impoverished, full of self-contempt and self-doubt. Negative mental tapes dominate their thinking, controlling their lives. "*If your daddy (or mama) couldn't love you, who do you think will love you? Nobody loves you. Nobody wants you. Nobody cares anything about you. Something's wrong with you. You're stupid. Ugly. Fat. You'll never find anybody to love you. What is there to love anyway? Blah blah blah blah blah blah blah blah.*" On and on the tapes blabber, chipping away at our self-esteem, destroying our chances at love and success. The truth about who we really are gets upstaged by the lies, abuses and hurts our wounded mother, father or other caregivers inflicted upon us long ago. That is, until we choose to face and heal it. Healing quiets those negative tapes.

4

WHILE HE SLEPT

There are homes you run from, and homes you run to.

LAURA CUNNINGHAM

Make two homes for thyself. One actual home and another spiritual home, which thou art to carry with thee always.

SAINT CATHERINE OF SIENA

I WAS DETERMINED TO GO TO SCHOOL. I NEEDED BUS AND LUNCH money, so at fifteen I started working. During the summer, I babysat my sister's newborn. That fall I got a real job at McDonald's as a cashier.

One brisk Saturday morning a little before dusk, I made my way home on foot. I'd worked the night shift, closed out my register, and helped clean until 4 a.m. As usual, none of the running vehicles outside waited for me. Nobody offered me a ride and shame mixed with pride prevented me from asking. All buses had ceased to run, so I walked. It was only a mile and a half, so I really didn't mind. Walking was meditative. It gave me time and space to think. This chilly morning, a towering forty-something year old man approached me, insisting that he see to it that I get home safely. The man mocked, "*You shouldn't be out here by yourself. It's dangerous.*" Unimpressed by his pretense of concern, I rejected his assistance and kept on trekking toward home. He persisted, insisted. I ignored him, hoping he would go away and leave me the hell alone. I hadn't asked for his help, didn't want it, and sure didn't need it. As I turned off of the well-lighted thoroughfare onto a dark side street—two blocks from the safety of my father's house—my tormentor stepped in front of me, put a gun to my face, then ordered me to the back of a building. My mind went into shock, deserting my body while my tormentor raped me. He finished, apologized, then walked into the gray morning. I ran home, quietly disrobed, discarded my clothes, scrubbed down my violated body parts, then sought the only comfort I knew I could count on—my bed. My parents lay sleeping across the hall, never the wiser. I saw no point in bothering them. What could they do? Besides, did they—meaning my dad—even care?

SHE'S COME UNDONE

Numbness replaced shock. I weep even now as I write this. Not for me, but for the lost and confused teenage girl I once was. That girl didn't feel protected or provided for, so she fended for herself. She handled the matter as best she could by shoving it to the back of her mind. That girl knew she had done nothing wrong. It wasn't her fault she was raped. She didn't deserve this violation. To her credit, she flat out refused to see herself as a victim, while understanding she had indeed been victimized. Whether good or bad, healthy or unhealthy, right or wrong, she forged ahead with her life as if nothing had happened. She sensed, even in her darkest hour, that she was blessed. It could have been worse, a lot worse. The rapist could have forced her to perform all manner of revolting sexual acts. He could have physically brutalized her, or worse, killed her. Now when I hear or read the details of a particularly horrific rape—such as that of the Central Park jogger—I marvel at the courage and resiliency such women must possess, knowing the degree to which they have suffered.

It was grace that saved me. Grace stood between death and me, wrapping itself around my essential self, my spirit—buffering me from shame, guilt and self-blame. Grace assured me that no matter what this man had done to my body, he could never defile my spirit.

My plan to keep the rape to myself unraveled when I came up pregnant. My brother Joel was furious that I'd not told the family sooner, denying him the pleasure of pummeling the culprit into the dirt. That made me feel good, to know my brother cared enough to get angry. Had I not known my mother, my father's reticence might have duped me into believing he didn't know what had happened to his seventh child. He never uttered one syllable to me about the incident. Maybe he felt somehow responsible, and shame had his tongue. What might he have said anyway? Well, he might have apologized for not picking me up from work. Or he could have told me he regretted having forced me to work. Perhaps he might have hugged me, for the first time, and told me that everything was going to be all right because he'd be there for me. He might have said or done any number of things. But, instead, he said and did nothing.

A week after I reluctantly told my mother about the rape and pregnancy, she snapped, "I don't believe you were raped!" Stunned and hurt by her words, I wept. How could she question me? Hadn't I been a good daughter, respectful and obedient— well, at least most of the time? Had she known me to be a liar? How could she think I was capable of fabricating such a story just to escape the mess I was in? Of one thing I am absolutely sure—my mother's sentiment emerged not from her rational, thinking mind but from an emotional, feeling place, where she felt afraid and powerless. There I sat, her daughter, three months pregnant, traumatized, in need of care, comfort and direction. "What do I do?" she undoubtedly wondered. That's a lot for any parent to face. It's doubly tough for a parent who's uncomfortable with feelings and shows of emotions, as my mother was.

WE ARE NEVER ALONE

There will be times when we feel desperately alone. We are never alone. Angels are all about us—some in the spirit realm, others earthly. Many are right in our midst, among family and friends. God knew my need. He knew that at such a dark time that more than anything I needed a confidant and comforter. He sent Ayo, my older sister by nine years, for me. After months of shouldering my nasty little secret in silence and fear alone, I finally had the ear of someone who believed me, someone who didn't blame me for what had happened to me. Ayo's care pulled me back from depression and despair. She reassured me that I was neither to blame nor damaged. In her quiet, nonjudgmental way, she queried me, "Was that your first time having sex?" It was not. I'd started having sex just months earlier. She was relieved, glad that the rape hadn't been my introduction to physical intimacy with the opposite sex. She tended my spirit. With her, I was able to talk about what happened to me, and to cry. My sister mothered me when my mother could not. I don't hold that against my mother. She did what she knew to do. The universe is so wise. It provides for our every need, often in unexpected ways. The people in our lives may hold one title but fulfill another role. Ayo acted as sister and mother to me. I needed them both.

Months prior to the rape, I had started having sex. I had a new boyfriend, Michael. Though my gut told me that the child growing in my 16 year-old belly was the rapist's, I had no way of really knowing this. It could easily have been Michael's. My mother, a devout Christian, had problems with ending any life. But she sensed what I knew; it would have destroyed my future if I were forced to daily face the rapist in the eyes and countenance of my very own child. It was unanimous. I would have an abortion.

My stomach had begun to protrude. My efforts to stuff it into my desk, to conceal it beneath baggy shirts was failing. People stared, some audaciously asked questions. I pretended not to notice the inquiring looks. I flat out ignored the queries. Everybody was on to me now. For three months, I had sought refuge in a state of denial, going about business as usual—home, school, friends, church. Not only had I dragged around my dirty little secret but now I was also pregnant. At sixteen I was but a baby myself. It was too much to bear. The pregnancy forced me out. But for it, I might have bore the burden of the rape in silence and secrecy all alone. We aren't meant to suffer alone.

One April morning, I ventured over to Johns Hopkins Hospital. That day, as I laid out on the cold, hard operating table flanked by a team of white coats, a baby lost its chance at life. A life which, until recently, I had never mourned for, so convinced was I that it had to end if I was going to move forward. We saw no other viable solution. Now that I'm a mother, I have thought about that child that almost was, have wept for it, and asked its forgiveness. It's regrettable that a life was terminated, but I shudder at the thought of what kind of mother I would have been at seventeen. As unfeeling as this may sound, I believe I did the smartest thing for us both—the unborn child and me. Birthing a child is easy—providing all that it needs emotionally, spiritually and physically is an entirely different matter. I was hardly mother material back then.

GYPSY WOMAN

Weary from the madness, a few months later, I fled my father's house. For a couple of years I lived akin to a gypsy. When I'd run into friends, they'd inquire, "So where you living now?" At the smallest infraction, I'd pack up my few valued belongings and move on. The day I escaped from my father's house, one of my older sisters invited me to live with her. When she shamelessly flirted with my boyfriend and withheld the bedding I'd been sleeping on, forcing me to sleep on her bare fake leather sofa, I moved out. When my girlfriend Denise squeezed her big bosomed torso into my size five clothes, without my permission, I thanked her family for taking me in, packed up my things and relocated. When my new "landlord," an old boyfriend, broke his promise not to put pressure on me for sex, I hit the road again. No place felt like home. Strangely, this didn't bother me much.

Some part of me knew I carried my home within me wherever I went. I was my strength, my comfort, my own security. I was free now. Free from ridicule, shaming, mistreatment. I left my father's house, the only home I'd ever known, to leave abuse behind. I felt completely justified in having zero tolerance for the slightest hint of maltreatment from all others. Sure, my hypersensitivity made me hyper-vigilant. Hypersensitivity and hyper-vigilance are normal responses to years of trauma and abuse. To the fragile wounded, they are forms of self-protection. However, as we recover our wholeness, we learn to set healthier boundaries. Then hypersensitivity and hyper-vigilance is replaced by self-respect and self-care. We don't bruise so easily anymore. Better still, we cease to put ourselves in glaringly dangerous or dishonoring situations. That is, we learn to take care of ourselves in ways that are proactive rather than reactive.

I graduated high school, on time. Thanks to my mother and more than a few extraordinary teachers whose belief in little DeBora Ricks pushed and pulled me through some pretty tumultuous times. *But now what? What do I do with myself now?* I wondered.

In my father's religiously austere house, there was no expectation that we go to college. It just wasn't something talked about. To be sure, there were expectations—though all largely unspoken. You were expected to go to school, graduate, get a job, live respectfully and—if my mother had the desires of her heart—you would not only know God for yourself but you would join her church of choice—the Church of God in Christ—and get and stay saved. Church took precedence over everything, school included. Interestingly enough, although I'd chosen to major in college preparatory in high school, I couldn't see college in my future.

5

THE SAILOR

The desire of the man is for the woman, but the desire of the woman is for the desire of the man.

MADAME DE STAËL

RAPE. PREGNANCY. ABORTION. ESCAPE FROM MY FATHER'S ABUSE. 1974 was not a good year. Yet, like a taut rubber band, the human spirit has the capacity to spring back. I turned my gaze forward, towards my future.

Life took an upswing. My girlfriend Denise's twenty-some-thing cousin, a young Miles Davis look-alike, swaggered confidently into my little world. Hailing from Virginia, where he was also stationed in the U.S. Navy, The Sailor was a ruggedly sensual man uncharacteristically comfortable in his own mocha-colored skin. I loved the sight of him. I imagined that he was just the kind of man that possessed the power to make me a woman. Secretly I'd feast on that cut, bared chest and belly that he casually paraded about Denise's house. But in no way did I entertain the unthinkable, that this delicious man could ever want *me*. So, without a fight, I surrendered him to Billie, my light skinned, big-legged girlfriend. Billie always managed to pull the hottest guys. I figured it was only a matter of time before The Sailor would make his selection public—and it would be Billie. She anticipated that day. We both mentally salivated. And worked hard to avoid appearing too interested or available—we would *act* natural, we decided without discussing it. I had no chance, I concluded. Truth is, it wasn't just about my competition. The Sailor was not like any other guy I'd ever met—he was, well uh, not a boy but a *man*.

Incredibly, he chose me! The Sailor chose me to be his girl. He chose me over Billie, a fact that rendered me deliriously happy, and her pissed. A man, a *real* man wanted *me*! I was happy—and scared stiff. At twenty-three, The Sailor was a man—mature, worldly. I was still the kid on the block at seventeen. I adored The Sailor way too much and myself much too little, which meant I not only permitted but invited his abuse, arrogance and chauvinism—the ice water hurled into my face, his substantial palm to my cheek, the frequent all niters with "the guys," the name calling. I was lucky to have such a prize, so who was I to expect that he would be all mine *and* good to me too?

DISAPPEARING ACTS

The Sailor and I moved in together. Then his disappearing acts increased even as his alibis grew lamer. I confronted The Sailor about his all-night escapades. As if I didn't already know, after one of our intense arguments, he confessed his sins—there was indeed another woman, "An *older* woman," he lied, as if the fact that she was a so-called "older woman" would make his cheating more palatable, less hurtful. But we survived The Sailor's infidelity. And mine's too.

Yes, I'd cheated. Once. The other man was a tall, gorgeous specimen who lived up the street, in the same apartment complex as we did. I cheated not for the thrill or variety of it. I cheated to recapture The Sailor's divided attention, to strike out at his over-inflated chauvinistic male ego, and to show him that two could play his game. Equally as important, I needed a fix. The new hunk's affections were enlisted to help me remember my

desirability as a woman, since I had trouble believing this without a man's help.

When The Sailor found out, (his cousin, my friend, Denise
told him because she secretly wanted this new man for herself)
he yanked me out of bed one sunny morning to give me a good
beating. This time, I fought back. Then I left him. Emotional
abuse I was well acquainted with. Physical battery was another
matter altogether. My daddy never hit my mother. Fist to flesh
was utterly intolerable. End of discussion. I drew a sharp line at
letting a man beat on me. My leaving was my way of sending
The Sailor an unequivocal message: *there would be no us if you
insist on hitting me.* For months he pleaded with me to come
back home. I held the doors of communication open, but for
months I refused his invitation to reconcile. Finally his promis-
es swayed me. I went back to him.

I moved back in with The Sailor, this time into a quaint, fur-
nished basement apartment across town. He broke it off with
the other woman and, as promised, never again laid a violent
hand on me. After our three-year tango ended, I would learn
The Sailor had a talent for brutalizing women, before *and* after
me. You might say his striking resemblance to the late great jazz
trumpeter was considerably more than what readily met the
eye—neither of them much valued women.

One day while The Sailor was at work, I left the house for a
long walk. I had no particular destination in mind, I just needed to breathe, think, feel, walk. This was an intensely lonely and
uncertain time for me. High school was behind me, but I could
see no future for myself up ahead. Or perhaps the amorphous
empty blob of time that stretched before me intimidated me,
since I had not one concrete plan for what to do with it. As I
made my way across a bridge, I paused at the guardrail where I
stood peering over. A truck filled with working men lumbered
over the bridge past me. One of the men yelled at the top of his
voice, "*Don't do it. Don't jump! Things can't be that bad!*" The
stranger's words shocked me. He'd echoed my sadness and con-

fusion. I'm not sure that I was seriously considering leaping onto the rocky stream below, if not to my death then likely to my disablement, but hopelessness had me in its grip. I'd been under the influence of a mild strain of depression for months. Though I had no real suicide plan neither did I have a prescription for living. I merely existed, floating on the river of life without any oars in the water. I had nothing to look forward to and I had no idea what to do with the next five, ten, fifteen years of my life. It was the hopelessness that I felt that stilled my feet on that bridge. That stranger's words shook me. I had to do something. I had to take charge of my life. I gathered myself together, turned and walked back home.

TAKING CHARGE OF MY LIFE

That evening, I sat The Sailor down for a talk. "I'm moving out," I informed him. "I'm going back home to my father's house. I need to go back to school, to college. I need to make a future for myself, so I've got to get a college education." "Can't you do that with me?" he pleaded. "No, I can't," I firmly insisted. I'd made up my mind, and there was no changing it. It was time for me to move on, to move forward on my own. The Sailor promised to support me however he could. Our lives never again intersected, except in passing.

I was twenty years old, working as a dietary aide for what we politically incorrectly called back then the "old folks home." The very thought of one day waking up forty years old still slaving in somebody else's hot kitchen terrified me. College frightened me too. But growing old with no marketable skills, feeling small and inconsequential because I'd neglected to get a college education scared me infinitely more. Two months after I moved back into my father's house, one summer afternoon while everybody was out he backed a U-Haul up to the front door, emptied the living room and moved uptown to a one-bedroom apartment. He deserted my shaken and bewildered mother and two younger sisters, who were ten and fifteen. He hadn't left me. He'd done that already, twenty years earlier.

College anchored my life, lending it contour and purpose. To think of it, school has always been the raft that kept me afloat amid the turbulence and chaos of my family life. I wouldn't be overstating it if I said school and the caring teachers that nurtured my mind and spirit possibly saved my life.

GATHERING MY THOUGHTS

The Sailor, and the time and circumstances we inhabited together, taught me many things. First, I mustn't underestimate myself. When he chose me over my friend Billie, I was pleasantly stunned. My self-esteem crept up a few notches. Something in me shifted, I considered that maybe I indeed had value. Before befriending Billie, I had been given no clear reason to doubt myself on the basis of the color of my skin, full lips, and large eyes. I was rather pleased with the face I saw in the mirror looking back at me. Boys seemed to like me, though not the popular football star types. Kind, respectful good guys sought me out. With Billie, I experienced my first taste of intra-racial color discrimination. I observed that most guys preferred girls with lighter skin, sharper features—girls who looked like Billie. This confused me. In my father's house, there was a rainbow of colors, from yellow to black with most shades somewhere in between. But nobody, so I believed back then, got elevated or denigrated on the basis of their hue. So all this color discrimination perplexed me. If you'd asked me, Billie wasn't prettier than me, just different. Neither better nor worse. I was the one with the hourglass figure, so one guy told me. But yet he asked for Billie's phone number. It took me some time to make sense of this. Interestingly, when Billie, Denise and I were out together, generally guys would pursue Billie first, then me, then Denise. Once I figured out that it was Billie's light skin that gave her the edge on me, it saddened me. I felt defeated, unfairly treated. But there was more at play here. Billie's advantage wasn't simply about skin coloring or even facial features. It couldn't have been, Denise was lighter than Billie. Billie had something more, personality and chutzpah. Billie believed fiercely in her feminine powers, and used them quite masterfully. At 17, she'd grasped the male mind. She understood men, that they are drawn to women who know they got the goods, are fascinated by women who think well of themselves, and are intrigued by women who know their worth. It wasn't uncommon for two guys to pay Billie a visit, simultaneously. Happily, she'd entertain them both. These were gorgeous, popular, sought-after guys who were used to winning in the dating game. For these guys, to be the first to hit the door would be to lose. So they stayed, and even seemed to enjoy the challenge.

When The Sailor picked me over the beguiling Billie, my sense of self took a quantum leap forward. From Billie, I learned to stand more firmly in my womanhood, to act as if, to test the waters. A few years later, after I'd moved back into my father's house, I did a Billie. Two enormously sexy specimens, Steve and Marvin, both vied for my affections. One summer evening, on my front porch, I entertained them both, and quite skillfully. I pulled it off simply because I believed I could.

The Sailor was the first man to make love to me. I'd had sex before, but never before had a guy considered my needs or desires. No one before had ever made sex feel like a demonstration of love—warm, passionate, tender, safe. The Sailor had. My pleasure was his pleasure. The Sailor became my standard, sexually speaking. Once a woman knows good loving, she is never quite the same.

Finally, with The Sailor, I saw the danger in valuing a man more than I did myself. The higher I elevated him above me, the easier it became for him to walk all over me. The greater the disparity in my perception of our worth, the more I invited his arrogance and abuse. My ability to respond to The Sailor's assault with my feet taught him—and me—that I can teach a man how to treat me, as long as I was willing to risk losing him.

6

SHADOWS IN THE DARK

We can't have the full experience of the light without knowing the dark. The dark side is the gatekeeper to true freedom.
DEBBIE FORD, *The Dark Side of the Light Chasers*

OUR BELIEFS DRIVE OUR LIVES. WHATEVER WE BELIEVE ABOUT ourselves shows up at our door. The reason we attract and create things, people and circumstances we insist we do not want is because our most powerful beliefs exist just beyond our conscious mind, embedded in our subconscious. If you were to ask the average woman what is it that she believes about herself, about her life, about her possibilities, she'd likely tell you what she *thinks*, wished she believed or what she thinks is the good and proper thing to believe. Truth is, most people aren't in touch with their deepest beliefs. We're afraid of what we don't know; afraid that what we don't know about ourselves is too ugly to bear. Thus we choose unconsciousness, leaving significant parts of ourselves in the dark—not only our weaknesses and flaws but also our perfect strength and beauty.

Trouble is, as long as toxic beliefs remain beyond our conscious awareness, we're doomed to sabotage our best efforts at love, work and life. For the lion's share of my adulthood, I was only dimly aware of a core belief that I felt unworthy of love. Meanwhile, my choices and decisions were driven by this conviction, creating chaos and confusion in my love life. On the one hand, I sought love. Yet when anyone dared to love me, I'd run or push them away. It took me more than a few failed relationships before I uncovered one of the roots of my problem—I fully expected every man I loved to desert me. Early on, of one thing I was sure—I didn't feel good in my skin. I didn't like me. I didn't love me. Yet, as do so many women, I hungered for the love of a good man. I imagined that if a man could love me enough, loving myself would be redundant. I was also convinced that my self-loathing could be remedied by something outside of me–a college degree, a career, a car, a nice home, a capable man. It would be years until I'd get it that *I first had to love me* before I could even let in or feel another's love. I would soon learn. But, of course, it would be the long and hard way.

SURRENDER DOROTHY

World-renowned Swiss psychologist Carl Jung observed that humans have a dark side, what he called "the shadow." In the shadow lurk the denied and disowned parts of ourselves, aspects of our psyche we deem unacceptable. We expend a great deal of life force—time, effort and energy—rejecting, repressing, resisting and resenting these parts of ourselves. Meanwhile these suppressed parts of us exercise a great deal of power in our lives. Despite our best efforts to succeed in love and life, our shadow beliefs can keep us from our deepest desires. They will, if we fail to acknowledge these beliefs and then integrate them into our personality, cleverly sabotage our efforts in love, finances, relationships and success. Since we can't escape the shadow personalities, we might as well recognize them. Accept them. Embrace them. Surrender to them. Love them. Integrate them. The beauty of integration is that our dark side plus our light adds up to one whole and therefore powerful force of nature. We start the process of integrating our shadow selves by acknowledging their existence, since we can't fix what we can't face. It's a process, one that takes courage and patience.

It wasn't until I got married, at twenty-eight, that I realized that something other than my conscious, rational thinking was impacting my intimate relationships with men. And it wasn't until then that I commenced the process of getting familiar with my dark side. But before that time, the love of my life, Chance, graced my life and brought his own wonderful, inimitable brand of light.

7

HERE COMES THE SUN

When you fall in love, you fall for a mirror of your own most present needs.

DEEPAK CHOPRA, *The Path to Love*

ON THE MTA BUS HEADED HOME FROM THE UNIVERSITY, Chance eased himself into my life. The semester was rapidly drawing to a close, summer fun hung expectantly in the air, and I was ready. I'd successfully navigated my first semester of college, and now felt confident that I was up for the challenge of college despite the horror stories that abounded about the black students who had dropped out of the University of Maryland. My strategy for staying the course to graduation was to take it one semester at a time. Except to pre-register for the upcoming semester, I would give no thought whatsoever to all the semesters and work that lay up ahead. This simple approach worked its magic. It alleviated unnecessary angst over what I lacked utter control over—the future and consequently left me with the mental energy and focus that I needed for the work at hand.

Chance was not on my romance radar. No man was. For three arduous months, school had been my possessive lover, and but for my part-time jobs, to it I was contently faithful. That day I initially saw Chance as just a lively conversation partner at the back of a bus. But I could feel his interested eyes heavy on me, his words directed at me. "This guy," I thought, "*likes* me." As we talked, the rest of the bus became background noise. Chance told me he'd been watching me, following me around campus, checking me out. "There's something special about you," he said. "You're so sexy." Despite the compliments, it bothered me that Chance was short, only a couple of inches taller than my 5'3" frame. I preferred to look up to my man. It didn't take long for me to learn that looking up to a man wasn't a matter of his physical stature but who he was inside.

Chance and I started going out. As our relationship blossomed, it became abundantly clear that whatever Chance may have lacked in height he more than made up for in strength of character, intellect, and charm. But it was Chance's magnetic energy that captured my heart. He had such a passion for and appreciation of life, a quality I'd never before witnessed in a man. He possessed a rare blend of brains, brawn and wit. Chance knew what he wanted, had a plan for getting it, and was fearlessly forging ahead toward it. He was the Man about Campus— a bold, dynamic leader respected by teachers and students alike. His talent for oratory thoroughly impressed me. Yes Chance was a man, a *real* man. The courage and tenacity he daily displayed was a beautiful thing to see in action. I came to think of him as the very embodiment of manhood. I had hit pay dirt.

SEX STRICTLY PROHIBITED

Interestingly, Chance bore a striking likeness to my father. He would be the first of a series of men who would. Their behaviors, attitudes, mannerisms, passions and even politics gave me the feeling of déjà vu. It really isn't all that remarkable that I attracted these men. Our deepest thoughts are magnets, drawing to us people and experiences that reflect our unconscious thoughts, memories and feelings. When our spirits linger in the past, we recreate the past in our present. We release the past through the healing practice of forgiveness, a gift I would eventually give myself.

Together, Chance and I leapt into the summer. We played tennis, ate Nation of Islam bean pies, bananas from street vendors, laughed, worked, took long drives, danced and fell in love. There was no sex. Not in the beginning. Chance was a dedicated martial artist, busy training for a regional tournament when we met. During training, sex was strictly prohibited. Years later, after bearing witness to the emotional blindness that premature sex often causes even a promising relationship, I appreciated the unexpected gift abstinence was to us. Because we kept our clothes on during the often pivotal getting-to-know-each-other phase, we unwittingly avoided a common relationship trap— confusing good sex with real love and worst, of all, reducing a beloved to the lowest common denominator—body parts. Ours was a soul connection. I wanted Chance so much I remember thinking I'd gladly hunker down with him in a cardboard box, if I had to, just to be with him. We were friends first, then lovers. I'd never had a friend in my lover. We genuinely liked one another. Our marathon talks kept us up all night, bouncing from politics to religion to relationships back to politics. I adored Chance's mind, so brilliant and robust. No other man had ever shared his mind with me, nor cared to explore mine. In Chance, I'd found a soul mate. With him life vibrated, simmered and soared. I was happy. Really happy.

For the flexibility in schedule and somewhat decent pay, I worked part-time as a cocktail waitress slash bartender throughout my college years. My debut gig was with a bar and lounge, G&G's in Edmondson Village. Chance would often pick me up at the end of the night, take me for a drive under the starlit sky, then deliver me safely to my door. At this time, I lived in an apartment with my mother, two younger sisters, and baby niece. Other nights I'd stay with Chance at his mother's east Baltimore row house. Fiercely protective, sometimes even downright chauvinistic, Chance made me feel cared for. With him, I felt safe, loved and respected. My soul was at home with this man.

8

JOE BOXER

There is a basket of fresh bread on your head,
and yet you go door to door asking for crusts.
Knock on your inner door. No other.

RUMI, *Persian poet*

I ADORED CHANCE. HE MADE MY HEART SING. THIS LOVE WAS
the closest I'd come to loving anyone unconditionally. Our lives
brimmed with light, laughter and love. Incredibly, I'd met someone so right for me, someone I loved and who loved me back. I
felt enormously blessed. In my beloved, I'd found a lover *and*
friend. Life was good. Then Joe Boxer, the busboy, came to work
at G&G's. A super jock—muscle bound, rough around the
edges, intellectually shallow—everything I abhorred in a man.
Not my type at all. Still I found myself strangely drawn to him.
Without explanation, I ditched Chance so I could date Joe, the
self-proclaimed ladies man with no intentions whatsoever of settling down with me or with any woman for that matter. We
never made it past mindless phone dribble. Thank God! But
what had I done? I'd broken Chance's heart to get with a guy I
didn't like, respect or want. A stud that cared nothing about me!
I'd irreparably damaged my relationship with the man I loved,
but why? We were so happy together. What was I thinking?
Where did this sick, inane behavior come from? What drove me

to trade in my well-designed Mercedes Benz for a buck wild Mustang?

Remember the shadow? Unconscious beliefs, facets of ourselves we can't live with so we repress and deny them? Well, one of my shadow beliefs was that I was damaged and therefore unlovable. Apparently my shadow had crept out to play. That's the nature of our hidden selves. They will surface, eventually. While out, my shadow cleverly orchestrated the circumstances that ejected Chance from my life. I wanted Chance's love, but I didn't believe I deserved it. I feared his getting any closer. I was sure that once Chance saw all of me, including the damaged, unlovable parts, he'd dump me. I injected Joe into the mix to keep Chance at arms length. Intimacy terrified me. When intimacy scares us, humans are known to indulge in all manner of subterfuge and sabotage to escape it. Not that Chance had been planning or even wanting to leave. He had been as predictable as he was thrilling. Still, he *would* leave. I was certain of that. Once he discovered who I *really* was, that I was not the woman he imagined me to be, he'd desert me. Why not spare us both the needless heartache down the road? I'll let go now. Jumping ship first had another "benefit," it helped my ego maintain the illusion of control in a situation that stirred up my fear of being rejected and abandoned.

TIT FOR TAT BLINDS US ALL

With Chance I'd suffered from happiness anxiety. This common malady, which afflicts people with low self-esteem, is cured by self-sabotaging behaviors that ultimately destroy our happiness, effectively redelivering us to a familiar status quo. Though the hurt that results may be worse than the angst of happiness, at least it's a familiar ache. The belief that we are unworthy of happiness, love and success keep us stuck in the pain of a familiar past. Want a cure for happiness anxiety? Raise your self-esteem. As your self-esteem grows, so does your capacity for joy, love and success. How do you boost your self-esteem? Endeavor to accept yourself unconditionally, especially those parts of you that you are tempted to deny, reject or hide.

Chance, at first, was devastated. But then, seemingly undaunted, he single-mindedly pursued reconciliation. We mended our love. By the fall semester, we'd reestablished our rhythm—school, work, shared time. Early one autumn morning as we enjoyed breakfast in the kitchen of Chance's gleaming new apartment, as the exquisite morning light shone across Chance's beautiful face something in my chest suddenly shifted. My heart had fallen. One moment I loved this man dining opposite me, the very next I was madly in love with him. I experienced a loss of control; my heart had slid out from my dominion right into Chance's hands. I was euphoric, and petrified. How would Chance handle my heart? I wondered. Even so, I'd messed up before with this lovely man, this time, I resolved, things would be different. I was in it, no matter what, for the long haul.

Love changed me. Protective walls came tumbling down. Boundaries collapsed. Chance's love shored me up. I was blissfully happy. Sadly, it wouldn't last.

A few months later, only days shy of Christmas, Chance dumped me. He phoned saying, "*I don't think we should see each other anymore.*" Click. My right hand reached for my chest to keep my shattered heart from tumbling onto the bed. I sobbed hard, loud and long. This was just a cruel joke. He's going to call back, in a few minutes, to tell me he didn't mean it, he was just kidding. Maybe Chance *did* mean it, but as soon as he realized his error, that he couldn't live without me, he'll call me back. He'd see that we were destined to be together, that I was his true love, his soul mate and he' would come for me. I waited. I prayed. I hoped. I waited some more but that call never came.

I'd hurt Chance. My early betrayal with Joe had damaging and lasting effects. I had destroyed the delicate trust that Chance and I had carefully cultivated. Chance struck back. Turns out that Chance got back with me so *he* could leave me. He wanted me to suffer like he'd suffered. So as soon as I fell madly in love with him, he walked out of my life. In one fell swoop, my world folded.

I believe now, as I suspected then, that Chance wanted to be with me as much I desired to be with him. However I had started something neither of us knew how to repair. I hurt him and he was intent upon hurting me. And he did, deeply. The old game of Tit for Tat. It's a deadly game, since inevitably all parties end up wounded. Yet it's the lethal weapon so many people reflexively reach for when they are hurting.

Wounded people wound others. Chance and I were emotionally and spiritually wounded. He loved me. I loved him. We loved each other as best we could love anybody. We, however, did not love ourselves sufficiently to sustain a healthy, resilient love. My fear of being abandoned dominated and controlled my life. The fearful mind chants, "*Don't trust him. Don't let him get too close. He'll just hurt you. Don't open your heart to him. He'll break it. He'll leave you. Leave him first. You've got to stay one step ahead of him. No, run!*" The ego mind, where fear reigns, is a wrecking crew. If we let it, the ego will sabotage our every effort at love. My beloved and I had unfinished childhood business that surfaced to be healed. Our conflict and chaos were invitations to grow emotionally and spiritually, invitations we naively declined.

HEALING UNFINISHED BUSINESS

The heart is pure. It wants, needs, gravitates toward love. It says, "*Ah, love. Open. Trust. Surrender. Love. You are loved. Lovable. You deserve to be loved. Let it in. Embrace it. Enjoy it.*" Our relationship thrashed about, fighting for its life. Despite repeated attempts to revive our love, once the romance broke down, we were never able to prop it up straight again. But the pure love that we had in our hearts, the love we'd tapped into when we first met, the love we desired but were too afraid to express— remained. Love, despite the form that the relationship takes, endures forever. Romance may fade, ebb and flow but genuine love never fails. My only regret is that like so many lovers, neither Chance nor I appreciated that the healing of our unfinished business was the reason why God had given us this time together. Had we known that, regardless of the length of our dance together, we might have moved with an open heart, embracing the bitter and sweet as opportunities for growth. But how many twenty year-olds appreciate that upon entering a new relationship they've signed up for a new class in the school of life? And then again, how many forty year-olds recognize this?

For five years, my heart grieved for Chance. Notwithstanding time and distance, a huge part of me remained hopelessly shackled to the conviction that Chance was my destiny, my soul mate, the man with whom I was supposed to pursue happily ever after. And for every one of those years, every poor unsuspecting guy I went out with got ruthlessly measured against Chance, the man who, like the sun, had lit up my life. Not surprisingly, every single one of them came up short. All but Jared. Jared helped me to expedite the process of relegating Chance to the lost love archives. Besides, by the time Jared had arrived, Chance was gone, married and living somewhere in the South. Life moves forward. It was time I went with it.

GATHERING MY THOUGHTS

With Chance, I discovered how fragile we are as humans. Men not excluded. We often handle one another harshly, seemingly unable to stop ourselves from hurting one another even when we know the pain our actions will bring. When we are hurting, if we aren't mindful, we spew our pain onto others, as if this will somehow alleviate our suffering. It doesn't. The shame and remorse that we feel in the aftermath makes us feel even smaller. Because we're all connected, the hurt I inflict on my brother boomerangs back onto me. It's a vicious cycle that only spirals downward.

Trust, I've observed, is the most delicate of human connective tissues. Once ruptured, it's impossible to repair unless the parties possess a healthy dose of self-esteem. High self-esteem gives you the strength of character it takes to own your part of the mess, and the humility to change it. Where there is no trust, love hides behind pretenses, defenses and walls. If trust is betrayed, love withers. Unless both people are willing to engage in the difficult work it takes to rebuild trust, love dies. A relationship where trust is absent is an emotional wilderness. Neither lover gets fed. My callous rejection of Chance destroyed the trust and consequently the love connection between us. Our relationship was irreparably damaged, but not because trust, once betrayed, cannot be restored. We simply lacked the self-esteem required to surrender the pretenses, defenses, and walls that can block love. For several years, we tried frantically to rekindle the fire but no amount of stoking would re-ignite it. We were simply too afraid of being vulnerable to surrender the protective armor we'd donned to shield us from further hurt.

Looking back, I can see how critical a role self-esteem played in the failure of my relationship with Chance. Neither he nor I possessed sufficient self-esteem to support true communion and connection. We'd made a soul connection but to sustain that connection we needed to like ourselves enough to risk emotional nakedness. We didn't. Once our fragile connection tore, we were at a loss as to how to mend it. Or perhaps we intuitively knew what love required of us, but were too afraid of ridicule and rejection to do it. Instead, we wasted precious energy and effort on blaming, shaming, resisting, hiding and struggling, none of which have the power to mend a broken love. These are the behaviors we engage in when we don't feel like we're good enough. On the other hand, people who feel good at their core are able to drop defenses, put aside pretenses, and lower walls because they know their character flaws and past failures neither define nor render them unlovable.

At least, with Chance, I discovered that a soul connection was possible with a man. In comparison, relationships I'd had that were just about the body were empty, lonely places. I knew, after Chance, that a man and a woman could indeed be both friends and lovers. For me, that was real good news.

9

No Talent for Dating

A strong woman is a woman who loves strongly and weeps strongly and is strongly terrified and has strong needs.

MARGE PIERCY

AS MY HEART GRADUALLY ACCEPTED WHAT MY MIND LONG knew—that Chance was never coming back to me—I embraced my lot. I was free to date. And so I dated, but badly. Meaning, if I was smitten by a man, I tended to think him worth keeping much too soon. I didn't know how to go out with more than one guy, simultaneously. I had no talent for dating. If a man liked me and I imagined that I loved him, I gave myself over to him in one fell swoop. Consequently I cheated myself out of the gifts that bona fide dating offers a woman, like the time to really get to know a man—and the power to *consciously choose* to be with a man rather than be chosen or fall blindly into a relationship.

What was my dating style? Well, I'd set my sights on the man I wanted (this after he'd sufficiently shown his interest in me), go out with him once or twice (maybe three times), then attach myself to him at the hip. Like a newborn to her mother's breast, I latched on for dear life. I lacked pacing skills. Perhaps that's why it's called *falling* in love. You can hurt yourself on the way down if you're not careful. At the outset, seldom was I careful.

College, the surest, most reliable ritual that I had in my life, ended unceremoniously. I'm not sure why, but I chose not to do the commencement thing. I simply took my Political Science degree and went to work. But for four grueling years, college had been king. There was nobody or anything more important than it, not even men. After Chance dumped me in my second semester, I shunned intimate relationships fall, winter and spring. I had no time, nor oddly, interest. Men became delectable summer pastimes. I share this because, quite honestly, I'm thrilled to be able to report that I, notwithstanding my love addiction, kept my priorities straight. Especially when I think about the countless number of women who have regrettably chosen a man over college, as did my best friend, who I'll call Janelle. The last week of her first semester at Morgan State University, instead of sitting for her finals, she laid up in bed with her deadbeat, near-do-well boyfriend. For obvious reasons, she never did get a degree. As emotionally wounded as I was, all my mental faculties functioned optimally when it came to my education. Education was my ticket to success and financial self-sufficiency. I considered it the height of insanity to think a man could supplant a university degree. I might have been a bit ill, but crazy I wasn't.

TWO HUNKS OF BURNING YUM

In the summer of 1983, I met Jared. Boy was he fiiiiine! He boarded the #3 bus and glided onto the seat next to me where I sat reading *Women and Feminism*. This was my last year at UMBC, my first introduction to feminism. I was living with my sister Ayo, the feminist who turned me on to this whole new way of thinking about women, men and power. As I read, well, tried to read, I could feel Jared's left arm lightly against mine. Attached to this hairy brown arm was a most beautiful male hand. In silence we rode toward our respective destinations. Yet between us hung a delectable electricity filled with romantic possibility.

Weeks went by. One Saturday night, again I took the #3 bus this time en route to a girlfriend's party in Charles Village. The bus was almost empty, with only about three to five people on board. Hearty male laughter pulled my attention to the front door. Two gorgeous, smiling men boarded the bus. "I know him, them!" excitedly I thought. "It's Marcus, uh, and with him is the stranger with the beautiful hands!" Marcus was a friend, he attended UMBC. The stranger was a friend of his. How n-i-c-e. Introductions were made. To my delight, Marcus and Jared decided to go with me to my friend's party. Things were getting interesting.

At the party, I was the envy of every woman, including my girlfriend Monica—who floated about the party like Zsa Zsa Gabor, her nose thrust into the smoky air, fingers clamped about a thin, dark cigarette pretentiously. Zsa Zsa brought her wealthy pedestrian sugar daddy with her. Except for a game of make-believe, there was nothing happening in their corner. Meanwhile, Marcus and Jared showered me with attention as they competed fiercely for mine. The three of us sipped on Sutter Home and Molson Golden as we talked and laughed about everything imaginable into the festive night. To say I had a great time would be superfluous. Women outnumbered men seven to one but lucky, lucky me, I had the good fortune to have two gorgeous hunks poring over me.

Jared asked me out. A week later, we met at a popular down-town haunt for drinks. I liked him immediately. He was a dynamo of male sensuality and energy, intelligently engaging and incredibly witty. Sparks flew. A romance commenced. Afterwards, Jared and I talked daily, often several times a day. Interestingly though, our natural affinity for one another never translated into sexual fireworks. Jared was still the sexiest, most electrifying man I'd met in years. In a word, he was magnetic— with a capital M. He enchanted, enthralled and excited *all* of my senses. Sex, I decided, was overrated. In any event, I felt certain, in time, good sex would come between Jared and me eventually.

BETRAYED

But things would not go well for Jared and me. Turns out, Jared *had* a woman. They'd been together for six turbulent years. One day, my younger sister Alverne called to tell me she'd seen Jared walking hand in hand with another woman in the Inner Harbor. Embarrassment and shame washed over me. Sure, he'd told me about her, right after our first night together. He'd also led me to believe they were drawing close to the end. That he was trying desperately to break things off with her. "But," he had groaned, "she needs me." His lying eyes then pleaded for understanding and patience. "She's so emotionally fragile. I just can't leave her right now. But soon. Give me a little more time." That was Jared's story, and he was sticking to it. Every approaching holiday gave him cause to delay—there was Thanksgiving, then Christmas, *her* birthday, *his* birthday, Ground's Hog's Day. You get the picture. Jared's "betrayal" made me feel stupid and small. Holding hands, to my understanding, wasn't a public display of affection men took lightly. A man doesn't hold the hand of every woman he dates or sleeps with. No, a man only reaches for the hand of the woman he adores, the woman he feels proudly connected to and protective of. Obviously there remained something worth holding onto between Jared and this woman, something he valued more than me. As I saw it, I was playing the fool and it was time to stop playing.

Though hurt, I decided there was no need for alarm, as usual, I had a bird in the bush. Since I never expected fidelity from any able bodied, red-blooded man, as a matter of course I kept a man or two in the wings. Enter Avery. I'd been seeing Avery for close to a year when Jared boarded my bus. Problem was, I couldn't decide if Avery was right for me. I knew I wasn't *in* love with him. Consequently, I always felt as if I was settling with him. Avery was so different from the kind of men who characteristically appealed to me. I gave Avery time and consideration because he wanted to be my steady man, my only man—

a fact he made crystal clear. I liked that he wanted me, that he had clarity about that.

Well, Avery was kind—or crazy—enough to accompany me to Jared's Mt. Vernon apartment to retrieve all of the items I've loaned him or conveniently left behind. Jared and I exchanged a few heated words before he released my belongings without incident as Avery stood silently by "his" woman's side.

PART TWO

STORMY WEATHER,
TROUBLED WATERS

10

MATRIMONIAL STRESS

Love and ego are incompatible. Surrender must begin on the smallest, most intimate scale. It starts with you and someone you love, learning to be together without resistance or fear.

DEEPAK CHOPRA

MARRIAGE NEVER TUGGED AT ME. IT WASN'T AS IF I WAS AGAINST it. It's just that it didn't beckon me. It simply held no promise or fascination for me. Unlike some of my girlfriends, my mind created no fairy tales fantasies about how blissful my life would be if only I had a husband. My parents' marriage undoubtedly had something to do with my jaded view of the institution. No paragon of passion or peace, their marriage had become a virtual battleground by the time I came of age. I bore witness to nothing but weighty silences, hostility and chaos. My father spent significant amounts of time on the road preaching the gospel or up in their bedroom preparing to preach it. Mother worked around the clock caring for her children and husband, with no apparent benefits or perks. Tenderness, touch and talk were like foreign languages—not spoken in my father's house. So you see, I had no cause to imagine that marriage would miraculously enrich my life. To be honest, if I desired anything from my parents' marriage, it was my father's power, control and freedom. In spite of me, I did inherit at least a few of my father's gifts, sorry to say, among them was a talent for crucifying my beloveds with a lethal, unmerciful tongue.

SOMEONE I CAN DEPEND ON

I first laid eyes on Avery in 1982, at a downtown bus stop. I was headed out to the University of Maryland Baltimore County, where I was entering my last year. His destination, I believe, was home from the Community College of Baltimore. His conservative, boyish good looks immediately captured my imagination. *Now*, I thought, *there is a man who can be trusted. Someone who would love me right, the way I needed to be loved. Someone stable, reliable, faithful. A man I could depend on.* Avery eyed me, shooting me that I'd-like-to-get-to-know-you-better glance. A week later, we bumped into each other at the Lexington Food Market. Destiny was knocking. We exchanged numbers. The following week, we did lunch. Our very different worldviews, Avery's obvious need for control, and my rebellious spirit made for a robust first date. Undaunted, we set a second. Then a third. I wasn't quite ready to get serious about any one man so I continued to see another guy I'd recently met, who coincidentally lived in the next block up from Avery. Avery pressured me to be with him exclusively. Because I saw Avery as a keeper and didn't want to risk losing him, I soon capitulated.

I began journaling in 1984, two years into my relationship with Avery. I can't tell you where my first book is now but, to date, I have over fifty journals of all shapes and sizes. I resorted to pen and paper when my sister Ayo moved to Jamaica with a white psychologist she met while vacationing there. I desperately needed someone to talk to—Avery had proposed and I wasn't sure I was ready for that level of commitment. My sister, my friend, my confidant, was gone. My journal would now be my confidant and refuge. I discovered that it also had a calming and clarifying effect on my mind. I got hooked.

In October 1985, in an intimate ceremony held at my sister Dorcas' gorgeous new home, surrounded by family and friends,

Avery and I tied the knot. It was during my marriage that journaling really took hold. Back then, I tended to journal only when my emotions were at extremes—happy or hysterical. For me, marriage felt like a daily roller coaster ride. There were many exhilarating highs followed by sudden lows. I wrote often.

FRIDAY, OCTOBER 10, 1986

It is now exactly one week away from my first wedding anniversary and Avery and I are very much apart in spirit. We just had another fight—one of so many. Most of them arise from ridiculous, trivial things. Tonight was one of the few times I felt unloved and undesired by him. All week he has been apprising me of the great number of women who would be delighted to have him. I can appreciate this. But am I to feel privileged merely to be in his presence? Once we got into bed, Avery turned from my kisses, continually insisting that I be quiet and go to sleep. Contempt for me was in his voice. It hurt. It still hurts. I sensed that he didn't care. I got out of bed to leave. This, as usual, resulted in an ugly scene. I eventually left. I'm now back, back home with my man.

RELATIONSHIPS ARE ASSIGNMENTS

Marital stress—Avery's expectations, wifely duties and demands, constant clashes—forced me, perhaps for the first time, to see who I became in a committed relationship. Maybe I had a hand in the success or failure of my love relationships. Up until then, I was solidly convinced that every one of my relationship miscarriages was somebody else's fault, specifically the man's. He was either a player, insecure, afraid of commitment, insincere, inadequate, scared, crazy, a dog or just the wrong one. Before family, friends and God, I'd promised to love, cherish, honor and respect ("to obey" was edited by the minister, at my request) this man through thick and thin until death do us part. Despite my best efforts, I couldn't pull it off. I tried. Avery and I both tried. And we both failed miserably. If anything, the more determined we were to make love work, the bigger a mess we made.

Our heroic efforts at making our marriage work were blindly misdirected. Avery was determined to control me. I doggedly clung to my autonomy. I set out to fix him. He naturally resisted. He demanded that I be less friendly, independent, free-spirited, self-interested. I pleaded with him to be more emotionally accessible, more confident and less rigid. Our we-need-to-talk sessions, almost always initiated by Avery, were cause for hope, signs of maturity—until they got underway and disintegrated into emotional heavyweight boxing matches. We'd batter each other with cruel, virulent words, play mind games, and overreact to innocuous words and gestures. Our talks were contaminated by what family therapist John Bradshaw calls "auditory hallucinations." Avery would hear things I hadn't said. Despite my insistence that he'd misinterpreted me, he'd cling to his skewed version. I'd routinely distort his words and behavior, secretly hoping to provoke him to confess his undying love and devotion to me. Largely, our reactions had nothing to do with the other, though it appeared that something said or done had triggered it. We were hopelessly shackled to our painful pasts. Like a deer transfixed by a set of glaring headlights, we were stuck in our respective pasts. Unfinished childhood business, negative mental tapes, real or imagined fears, past traumas and hurts were the language we shared. Blinded by our fears, we didn't even see each other—only who we imagined the other to be, someone from our past who had badly hurt us, someone poised to do it again.

Authentic communication requires a healthy measure of self-esteem, since it demands honesty, transparency and the willingness to be emotionally vulnerable. In true communion, we suspend and at times surrender our ego to understand and to be understood. We offer our beloved our authentic, vulnerable self, trusting that whatever unfolds we can handle. To enter into true *commun*ication is to open oneself to the possibility of being changed by the exchange. "To have communion," bell hooks writes, "is to be willing to be honest, for communion is predicated upon the genuineness of interaction between two people." Genuineness of interaction demands a sense of one's self as okay, a wisdom that neither Avery nor I possessed. Yes, we talked perpetually, but we rarely communicated.

Trauma has that affect on you. Someone summed it up this way: *until you heal your source relationship—meaning that troubled relationship with that problem parent—you are never really in a new relationship.* Which meant Avery was my unloving, controlling father. And I was his mother, an ambitious, self-centered woman with a genius for deceit, someone he distrusted deeply.

Relationship is not about shielding yourself from loneliness, nor is it about having someone to pool your resources with so you can pay for your dream house, luxury cars, and exotic holidays. "Relationships are assignments," says Marianne Williamson in *A Return to Love.* They are workshops, classrooms and laboratories for learning. Your beloved is in your life to help you see more clearly into you, into those dark, dank nooks and crannies of pain, shame, blame, anger and fear. Your beloved forces your shadow sides out and onto center stage for integration and healing.

SATURDAY, OCTOBER 18, 1986

Last night was one of the most beautiful nights of my entire life. It was my first wedding anniversary with Avery Greene. I'm in love. In fact, the feeling of love for him is almost overwhelming. He sent a dozen long stem red roses to my job. I was surprised near tears. As I talked to him on the phone afterwards, I did cry. I cried because that was the only thing left for me to do. God, I thank you. Avery is your way of showing me your love. God, help me. You have blessed my days and nights with this man's presence. Guide me. Show me how a good woman keeps a good man happy. My love, heart and body are his.

11

KILLING ME SOFTLY

body slam you to the ground,
messaging a chill
curses make the head go 'round,
brings a certain thrill....
and it's supposed to be love...

ABBEY LINCOLN, *jazz singer*

MY MARRIAGE BEGAN TO TAKE A TOLL ON MY HEALTH. I HAD
sleepless nights followed by exhaustingly tense days. A lump the
size and feel of a walnut lodged itself in the center of my throat.
I figured it was stress induced. But how could stress feel so real,
so tangible? The lump persisted. I made an appointment to see
a doctor. I refused to believe something so palpable could be all
in my mind: there simply had to be something medically wrong
with me. For an entire week, I suffered. My insomnia also continued, three or four nights, I slept but a wink. Misery became
my constant companion. Saturday morning, Avery flew down to
North Carolina on a business trip. From Saturday until Monday,
I enjoyed sound, restful nights of sleep. The walnut dissolved. As
the time to retrieve Avery from BWI neared, the lump returned.
Avery's love is *killing me*, I thought.

Our bodies register emotional pain, warehousing it in our
muscles, cell tissue and organs. Louise Hay lists in her book, *You*

Can Heal Your Life, physical illnesses and their corresponding mental and emotional roots. According to Hay, throat problems indicate a stifled, repressed voice. I, the proverbial *independent black woman,* was repressed? Could I possibly be guilty of choking down my words? I spoke my mind. I didn't hesitate to tell Avery what I thought. I wasn't shy or timid about telling him what I wanted or needed. But what about my heart, was I speaking up for my heart in my marriage? Better still, did I even know my heart's needs or desires? No, I didn't. Or perhaps I did know but I was too opposed to being alone to give them voice. My authentic voice, thin and emaciated from inattention bordering on neglect, was buried beneath an inauthentic life I lived to avoid taking full responsibility for myself.

Medical tests confirmed it—I was physically healthy. The lump in my throat was caused by the stress in my world. If I could eliminate the stressors, my body would heal itself.

PSYCHIC READING

Yolanda, an attorney on my job, had gone to see this woman, a psychic. The woman, she insisted, had the ability to read people. Growing up, my mother had filled my head with haunting stories about unsuspecting individuals back in Bassett, Virginia (her hometown), who had become the unfortunate target of a spell cast by, say, a betrayed wife or jilted lover that was purchased from some able voodooist. Convinced that nothing good could ever come of it, early on I vowed never to seek such folks' counsel. "Besides," my mother insisted, "good Christian folks have no need for black magic—we have Jesus." But Yolanda talked so *highly* of the woman, she piqued my curiosity. And, of course, I was desperate for answers.

In the meantime, Jared had resurfaced. I was secretly spending evenings with him after work, indulging sinfully in his tenderness, sweet kisses and adoring words. I was torn, not only between two men, but more significantly between known suffering in a rapidly disintegrating marriage and the possibility of unknown happiness if I could bear to leave it. I needed some concrete answers.

I threw my mother's caveat to the wind and went to see the woman. She was a portly white woman about forty years old with a round, friendly face framed by a wild head of red hair. I handed her a crisp $20 bill, took the chair at the table across from her, then waited to be wowed. She informed me of my marital status, as she arranged and rearranged the colorful cards on the table. Nothing supernatural about that, there was a half carat diamond ring with a matching wedding band on my left ring finger. Yawn. I was *not* impressed. She blabbered on, telling me that there was not one but two men in my life. That one had a child, a daughter, about ten. "You care for both men, but you don't really want to be with either," she informed me. "In fact, you don't want to be married at all. Nor do you truly wish to make a life with the other man." All true. She was right on point. But still I had reasonable doubt. "You," she casually added, "have a lump in your throat." I sat up straighter in my chair. How could she possibly know this? There were absolutely no apparent indications of my condition. It was completely an internal thing. Yolanda hadn't told her, since I'd never discussed my marital woes with her.

The clairvoyant's ability to "see" my pain confirmed my suspicions, giving me the kick I needed to accept and embrace my inner reality—I deeply needed to be alone with myself. Not simply because I was unhappily married, but my soul hungered for a deeper, richer relationship with me. Intuitively I knew, as long as I had a man in my life, I'd manage to keep devising ostensibly legitimate reasons for not steadily exploring and mining my own inner landscape. Until I gave myself the gift of charting life solo—at least for a significant period of uninterrupted time— my spirit would be unrelenting in its pursuit of some undivided, quality time with me.

I loved Avery, to the extent that I was capable of loving anyone back then. I nonetheless remained conflicted, caught between my desire for security and my soul's longing to evolve. My belief, an insidious shadow, that I was nothing without a man, continued to hold sway over my life, trumping decisions that would have served my highest and best good. My heart and soul longed to experience the freedom of the single life but I wasn't developmentally ready to be without a man just yet. I chose to stay with my husband.

12

UNFAITHFUL

*As long as there are parts of yourself that reach outward to make
you feel safe, valuable, and loved, you need to identify them and
heal them.*

GARY ZUKAV & LINDA FRANCIS, *The Heart of the Soul*

TRAVELING IS ONE OF MY SWEETEST PASSIONS. DETERMINED TO
see as much of the world as time and money would permit, and
bent on maintaining some semblance of my autonomy in my
marriage, I flew to Atlanta, Georgia with my best friend, Janelle,
for a long Halloween weekend. We had a heehaw good time,
starting with our flight down. Still giddy from the cognac we
threw down while airborne, Janelle and I were picked up by
Buffy, my Atlanta friend and delivered to our quaint downtown
hotel. Once there, we cracked open a bottle of champagne for a
toast. Buffy then left for a prior engagement, leaving Janelle and
I on our own that evening. We showered, dressed and took a taxi
to a nightspot several blocks away. We had the good fortune to
meet two attractive men at the club. We danced, flirted, laughed
and made plans to hook up the next evening. The weekend was
on!

That Saturday, we went with our two new hunks to a cos-
tume party. We saw them again at lunchtime on Monday, before
our scheduled flight home. We got so caught up in our good-

byes, having just one more for the road, that we missed our four o'clock flight by five minutes. We were on the next flight five hours later.

I returned home, late that evening, renewed, happy and horny. Thrilled that I had a man waiting at home for me, I bounced down to baggage claims where Avery waited impatiently. All was well in my world. I was looking forward to nightfall and loving my man. When I crawled into bed next to my guy, he demanded, "Swear on the Bible that you didn't sleep with anyone while you were in Atlanta!" "No!" I shouted. He persisted. "Tell me you didn't go to bed with anybody while you were away. I need to hear you say it!" I was physically exhausted and emotionally fed up with this insecure man's chronic need for reassurance. I thought, if we aren't going to make love, then I am going to at least get a good night's sleep. So I lied. "Okay, you win, I *did* sleep with somebody. I slept with this guy I met at a Halloween party on Saturday. Now, are you *happy*? The dark room got quiet. I could hear Avery thinking. "I don't know if I should be pleased that you finally told me the truth or should I go to the kitchen and get a butcher knife and put it in your back." Avery mutters in a forceful, cold voice. A knife would have been superfluous, I thought. His words had cut right through me. Quietly I sobbed. I wondered how could the man who vowed to cherish, love and stand by me entertain brutal thoughts of killing me? I told him I'd fabricated that story to shut him up, so I could get some sleep. "Now I believe you," he mumbled, "since you were willing to risk lying about being unfaithful. I'm so sorry. I apologize for what I said." Despite Avery's profuse apologies, he'd inflicted a near fatal blow to my heart and our marriage, which was already hanging dangerously in the balance.

EMOTIONAL INFIDELITY

I was no victim. I betrayed my man's trust, this time my husband's, the man I'd promised to love and honor. To be sure, there is a multitude of ways to be unfaithful. Sexual exploits are only the most obvious. No, I hadn't slept with any other man. But yes, I had been unfaithful. I'd sat on another man's lap and kissed him. I'd felt feelings for this man that should have been reserved for my spouse. I had been untrue to my husband, my marriage, and my vows. Yes, I had cheated on my man, unequivocally.

I offer no excuses for infidelity. Nonetheless, for the emotionally dependent woman, there are reasons why they fail to honor commitments in love. Infidelity was not the problem, but a symptom of a deeper affliction—addiction. I was addicted to the attention and approval of men. Any man. Men were my drug, quick fixes. I turned to men for validation, identity and meaning. I lived off their approval, craved their attention. I felt insufficient alone. I reached for a man when I felt powerless, weak or afraid. A man's affection was like money in the bank, the more of it that I got the more confident I felt, if only momentarily. I hated, no, feared being alone. It frightened me, more than death itself. In fact, aloneness was a kind of death for me. Alone I seemed to disappear, to become nothing. So I avoided aloneness at all cost. I hoarded the affections of men, in case one should misbehave, leave or ignore me. And so at twenty-eight, I was no more emotionally ready for marriage than a nine year old. I cared for Avery, but I married him for all the wrong reasons–to escape aloneness, to ensure a regular dosage of male approval, and for help in making my dreams come true.

Though I desired closeness with Avery, I was conflicted. My discomfort with emotional intimacy and fear of ending up alone drove me to scatter my affections about to two or three suitors so as to ensure a steady, seamless flow of attention and adoration. No one man was up to the task, therefore I filled up on "love" wherever it appeared to beckon. Ostensibly a self-supporting woman, still I had yet to learn the art of filling my own emotional tank.

Sunday, January 11, 1987

The only time Avery and me can go off separately is when we have been fighting. And we fight all the time. Mostly we fight about what wrong thing I've done. Just recently while I showered, he read my journal, violating my privacy. It seems he's set on controlling me, changing me. His goal? To mold me into the kind of woman that he thinks I should be, the kind of woman who builds her world around him, shutting all others out. His frustration is that I'm not cooperating.

Monday we fought about Avery reading my journal. We made love that night. Tuesday, Wednesday and Thursday are somewhat of a blur. He studied for his accountant's exam. I shampooed my hair. We interacted. We loved each other. There was harmony in our home. We still had each other. The world was sweet. Friday, I went out with Terri. We had fun. I got in at 4:30 a.m. Saturday morning. Avery didn't reveal his anger when I got home. I was terrified, like a child who didn't come straight home from school. I knew I'd be punished. But we made love. Passionate, greedy love. When I awoke Saturday afternoon my husband, my lover, was gone. This is Sunday evening, now Avery isn't talking to me.

Avery and I would do our song and dance of guarded closeness followed by chilled distances. Unless a fight preceded it, we had the hardest time heeding Kahlil Gibran's advice to "put some space in your togetherness." Avery and I had trust issues. Issues that existed long before we married, before we met, dating back to our childhood and previous relationships. I did not trust men. Reared by his mother under a cloud of mystery, deception and lies, Avery had a deep mistrust of women. We wanted to trust. We just lacked the capacity to do so. We were much too broken inside.

Emotionally healed individuals are comfortable with closeness and time and space between them and their beloved. They celebrate their individuality. In touch with a self that they like, healthy lovers can open up to their beloved and let themselves be seen.

WEDNESDAY, MARCH 18, 1987

I told Avery that I'm leaving. Since I've threatened to leave before when he and I both knew I didn't mean it, he now doubts me. I truly mean it this time. Our relationship is dying. We no longer enjoy each other. Nor are we passionately fighting anymore. My heart isn't in it. I no longer desire to be here. The joy is gone.

Let me think back to our first meeting. Our arguments have remained the same. He wanted to be everything and everybody that I needed. I wanted to continue to enjoy others. We battled. I remember once when I lived on Eutaw Place he came over demanding that I spend more time with him or he would end the relationship. I hadn't seen him in three days. He decided that it had been too long. Another time I had planned a nice, warm Friday evening with Avery at my place. He got there. We sat on the floor talking. About 11 p.m., the doorbell rang. I went and came back from the door in less than five minutes. For two to three hours Avery badgered me. It was so unnecessary. His argument was that it was too late for any man to just pop up at "his" woman's place. He spoiled the entire night with his stupidity.

Anyway, we're just two lovely people together who are unsuited for one another. In other words, we're incompatible. I love Avery but not enough to forgo my desire to live completely. He wants me to sacrifice and compromise. I refuse.

MONDAY, APRIL 6, 1987

Nothing particularly exciting or interesting happened today. It's very peaceful here. Avery isn't home. Our relationship is a continual source of pain. We're embracing one moment, denigrating one another the next. We need therapy if we're going to keep loving one another. It's getting more difficult by the argument. He wants more time together, more sex, more common goals, more commitment, and I want more time alone, more space, more individuality, more self-control. And the beat goes on. We argue about the same issues daily. He says I never give enough. I say he wants too much. We are so different. My spontaneity is my way of getting joy out this life. He's a planner—rigid, inhibited. I still love the person he is, but our personalities often clash.

The more I write the more concerned I get. Those things that brought us together threaten to end our marriage. He's idealistic. I'm realistic. We can't merge. We have real differences. Either we accept our differences or we separate. I love Avery but I want so desperately to live a full, free, spontaneous life. He wants to place limitations on me. I constantly rebel. Often I rebel too much.

TUESDAY, MAY 12, 1987

A lot has happened since I've last written here. Avery and I decided to stay together. One night we took a walk to the park. We talked. Really, in retrospect, I talked. He agreed or occasionally commented. We embraced and hugged a lot. It felt good. It felt right. When the two of us got back home, we made love for the first time in months. He all but begged me to stay afterwards. I cried uncontrollably because I knew I had to make a choice that I could live with. Deep inside I feared that I hadn't given my marriage my all. I feared that leaving right now would incur the wrath of God. A few days later, Friday, I decided to stay so I unpacked and set up house again. It wasn't an easy decision at all. I've been making some great spiritual strides. Although I've experienced a considerable amount of instability in my love relationship, I'm getting centered. The books, plus Evergreen's Adult Children of Alcoholics meetings and people, have positively impacted upon my life. Self-love and acceptance isn't the task it used to be.

13

TELLING OUR STORIES

*If you bring forth what is inside you, what you bring forth will
save you. If you don't bring forth what is inside you, what you
don't bring forth will destroy you.*

JESUS OF NAZARETH, *The Gospel of Thomas*

*Only one thing is more frightening than speaking your truth.
And that is not speaking.*

NAOMI WOLF

WE ARE GUIDED. ALWAYS. GOD LOVES US SO MUCH THAT HE
engages in a myriad of ways to get our attention, always with the
goal of steering us through the darkness into the marvelous light.
Our intuition, passions, desires, hopes, dreams, longings and
fears—if honored—will lead us back to our wholeness. When
we nobly pursue a particular job or avocation with the good
intentions of improving the lot of another, I believe we are firmly on the path to our own enlightenment. Our work reveals us
to ourselves. It illuminates areas of our lives in need of healing—
for as they say—we teach what we most need to learn. Every job,
like every soul, is our teacher—there to help us evolve spiritually. There are no accidents. Every job is significant, no matter the
title, position, duties or pay. What impels us to a particular pro-
fession is as much about what we stand to gain as it is about
what we ultimately give. Life is but a series of relationships—

relationships with people, things, ideas and activities. Work is one such relationship.

October 1983, I went to work in the newly established State's Attorney's Office Domestic Violence Unit. As a paralegal slash advocate, it was my job to prepare criminal complainants, who were 95% women, for trial. Among the many referrals I made, I'd routinely urge complainants to attend one of the many Twelve-Step programs offered in their communities. After years of steering other women toward healing their codependency issues, it occurred to me that I could better serve my clients if I had first-hand knowledge of these programs. One Sunday morning, in the spring of 1987, I did just that. I went to an Al-Anon meeting on the campus of Loyola College, affectionately called The Evergreen. The next Sunday, I wandered into an Adult Children of Alcoholics (then ACOA, now ACA) meeting. Finding a space on the crowded floor, I sat enthralled by the participants—white, black, female, male, wealthy, struggling—who bared their souls speaking the truth of their lives. I got hooked. I'd found myself at home. All those years I'd searched for God in a church and when I wasn't even looking, I stumbled upon Her in a room full of people dedicated to healing their lives by telling their stories.

FORGIVING MY FATHER

For the next five years, I religiously attended Adult Children of Alcoholics meetings at least twice a week. Next to forgiving him, it was the most pivotal step towards healing my relationship with my father that I would take. Initially I just sat and listened. Then I began to tell my story, about my painful relationship with my father. Thoughts, feelings, and solutions spilled from me that I didn't even know lived inside me, like the resentment I felt toward my mother for not protecting me from my father. I got to talk uninterrupted, laugh out loud at myself, and cry like a baby. With nobody to judge me wrong for what I thought and felt, I came to trust and validate my own reality. That's an important, critical step in recovering ourselves—we've got to trust that what we feel and know is okay to feel and know and that all of it has value.

One of the things that the African American community wrestles with is the notion that our mothers—and fathers for different reasons—ought to remain beyond reproach. This need to see our mothers as a sacred cow, so to speak, keeps countless people in the dark about the root of their self-loathing and addictions. If you doubt me, look as I have for an Adult Children meeting in the black community. If you find one, rejoice. "*Hate your mother, hate your father*" meetings, as they were sarcastically called by many Narcotics Anonymous members, were rare in our communities twenty years ago. I can recall but two. I felt I had no choice but to attend the predominantly white middle-class Adult Children meetings if I was going to get well. The more we can speak the truth about our life, the better our chances are of healing the lies that bind us. As long we keep the truth of our life beyond our conscious awareness, we live in fear. It might help to remember that nothing that is human warrants a lifetime of shame and hiding. Give yourself the gift of self-examination. Own what you find. Accept it whether or not you like it. Then work to integrate or discard it.

We are not talking about blame here. To blame is to make someone else wrong. We do not make our parents bad by acknowledging their part in our development. I, however, have met too many people grappling with unaddressed pain from childhood that could easily be healed if they could only accept that their mother or father hurt them. Interestingly, the more I confessed the truth of my relationship with my dad, the more I was able to see his humanity and forgive him.

14

SELF-MEDICATING

You cannot begin the work of releasing an addiction until you can acknowledge that you are addicted. Until you realize that you have an addiction, it is not possible to diminish its power.

GARY ZUKAV, *The Seat of the Soul*

MONDAY, JULY 13, 1987

Much is going on in my life right now—most are inner activities. I'm becoming more in touch with the God in me. I've virtually stopped drinking alcoholic beverages. The desire is no longer with me. I seldom give myself enough compliments but I sincerely deserve a pat on the back for having achieved this feat. Alcohol had become a staple in my life. I remember how and when I picked up the destructive habit. In 1983, both Avery and I worked downtown. At the time, I was doing volunteer work with the State's Attorney's Office. Every evening just about, Avery and I would go to a bar and drink like fish. Every social outing included liquor, specifically beer, and sometimes wine. We spent a lot of time inside bars. The weekends would be more of the same. Some days, especially Sundays, I would awaken, look in the mirror, and loathe the face I saw. My eyes were dark circles, my skin had lost its luster, and I need not mention my breath. Although we may have made passionate love the night before, I couldn't remember a single detail. Avery and I both grew concerned. We wondered if we were alcoholics.

To this day, I don't know. But I do know that I made a conscious decision to become far less reliant on booze for my ups.

So, I suppose, this is where my urge for greater spirituality crept in, the desire to know the God within now had a sober house in which to dwell. You see, alcohol for many people is the one thing that they can count on to make them feel—feel good, sociable and relaxed. We attempt to drink self-esteem. We desperately strive to feel whole and complete. We want to fill the empty spaces in our lives and person. But nothing as potentially destructive as booze could ever create true joy. Most of us become addicted before we realize this. This, however, may be the one thing that will lead us to a spiritual awakening.

I don't believe one can be perpetually drunk and spiritual at the same time. Spirit is totally fulfilling. The need for anything destructive declines proportionally the more our lives embrace the light. This is what I'm experiencing right now in my life.

I've started running again. And, thank God, there is no knee pain. I run early in the mornings through Druid Hill Park. This morning as I ran, I asked God to let me see things, people, his creations as if seeing them for the first time. I noticed the moon during the day. And oh the sun was extremely beautiful as its bright orange and yellow rays of light filtered through the looming tree branches. As I gazed at the sun, I started to cry. I thanked God for all things. I'm transforming. Those things and people that I need come unto me.

This weekend Ayo and I participated in a self-awareness workshop given free by students of guru Sri Chinmoy. It was essentially meditation. I gained peace as well as information. I bought two books and a beautiful tape all by Sri Chinmoy.

15

STERLING SHINES

Ah, the relationships we get into just to get out of the ones we are not brave enough to say are over.

JULIA PHILLIPS

STILL MONDAY, JULY 13, 1987

    He sat behind me, watching me. I glanced his way, noticing him but pretending not to. He ate and talked. His energy is still fresh in my mind. It moved me. When the meeting ended, he hugged me, as others did. His eyes were emerald green, clear. Later he told my sister that he wanted to know me. It felt good to be desired. I smiled. He'd often tell my sister nice things about me. It was inevitable that we would talk. The energy was there. I'm moved by a man's energy. The first time we talked, I was uneasy. The next time was warm, easy. If only the conversation didn't have to end. Once off the phone, his presence remained with me. Is it infatuation?

    I stand at the top of the steps outside the Evergreen building on Loyola's campus, waiting for him. Sterling walks up. I stare at his very handsome, bearded face, into his green eyes. His body is loose, sexy, relaxed. His shirt is buttoned halfway up, that mixed gray chest hair exposed, teasing me. His appeal is incredibly strong, undeniable. I want him. I'm glad he came to meet me. Later we walk and talk. In the park, we sit. I gaze into his eyes trying to touch whatever lay behind them. He's a man. I'm a woman. I like it. I like it a lot. As we cross the street, he reaches for my hand. He's very much a man. I like that. We talk about feelings. He confesses that he prays, says he tells the truth even when it might hurt. At his place, we talk more and some more. I tell him that all that I really want right now is some tenderness. He pulls me to his lap. "You're hot," he whispers. I know. "Are you always this hot?" he wants to know. I don't answer. He holds me like a man is supposed to hold a woman. I want him. Our hands play together. We kiss. I moan. My body is screaming for him. He's a man, all man. And I want him. I pull away because the dream should end. But it continues when we stand face to face. He wraps his powerful arms about me. My face falls onto his beautiful chest, just below his chin. I kiss his neck. He feels so good. I hold on. I don't want to ever let go. But I had to. I was still a married woman. I managed to extricate myself from this beautiful man, before things got any further out of control, before I bedded him that night. He saw to it that I got back home to Avery, my husband.

ADDICTIVELY REACHING FOR ANOTHER

I was intensely attracted to Sterling. All that was woman in me wanted this man. That Adonis physique, that sparkling white smile, those emerald green eyes! Though stunningly sexy, the man seemed completely oblivious to his good looks, making him all the more beautiful. Blessed with every reason to be arrogant and self-absorbed, Sterling nonetheless was decidedly modest and internally directed.

I thought well of Sterling, admired his commitment to honesty and recovery. I enjoyed being with him, hanging out and talking. I especially loved the hot and delicious sex we made every chance we got. I was tempted to call what we had love, but I secretly knew it was lust and need that melded our lives together. That is the unsavory nature of addiction, whether to relationships, men, drugs, shopping, drink, sex or gambling. Stress, problems, feelings of powerlessness, fear and low self-esteem can trigger addictive behavior, even before we realize that we're caught in its grip—yet again. My marriage was hard and turbulent. Trying to make love real—and failing miserably—managed to kick up my fear of abandonment. I didn't want to be alone. Sterling made me feel beautiful, bolstered my ego, and gave me someone other than me and my pain to focus my efforts on. He was the safety net I demanded if I was going to leave my marriage, something that was becoming glaringly inevitable.

Feelings of powerlessness were triggering my addiction. Rather than sitting still and feeling my pain, I was running from it, straight into the arms of my most potent pain reliever, a man. Being the object of an appealing man's desire always gave me such an incredible, delicious rush, making me feel beautiful, powerful and in control. The more delectable the man, the greater the value of his desire. The greater the number of appealing men in pursuit of me, the more valuable I believed myself to be. Look at who *wants* me, my addiction lied. I *had* to be something.

I was using Sterling, treating him little better than a dope fiend treats a vial of cocaine. It was all about me, my desperate need to avoid being alone with myself. My marriage was rapidly approaching a nasty end, as evidenced by the emotional cease-fire Avery and I were under. Being alone simply was not an option I'd *ever* entertained. Sterling would serve as a means to an inevitable end, separation from my husband.

Monday, August 10, 1987

A lot of changes have occurred since I've last written here. On August 1st, Avery moved out. The night before, I stayed with Sterling. We'd spent most of the previous day, Saturday, going to Twelve-Step meetings. On Sunday morning, I took the elevator up to the eighth floor, to my apartment. Sterling went to the store across the street. As I approached my front door, I had this strange feeling that Avery had moved out. I cautiously opened the door. My suspicions were confirmed. The place was a wreck. In my excitement and fear that Avery had taken some of my belongings, I rushed down to the lobby for Sterling. I soon learned that the TV, stereo, VCR, coffee and end tables, bed and oriental rugs remained. Avery did take a few of my belongings, items I'd brought into the marriage, and every one of his. I was afraid to do a thorough check for fear of getting really angry about my losses. Sterling asked me if I wanted to cry. Crying was far from my mind. All I felt was shock then relief. After all, I had planned on leaving on September 1st. For the last couple of weeks Avery had witnessed me pack for a trip to Nassau that never happened. I think he had been convinced that I was preparing to leave him. I had also removed the sheets from the bed and rugs from the bathroom and washed everything. That's my pattern when I'm about to move. He undoubtedly figured he'd beat me to the punch. Must have been a last minute impulse, because the last thing Avery wanted to do was make life easier for me. After all, August 1st rent had been paid. That was truly a blessing. Later I learned that, in vain, he tried to get management to give him the rent back. If the rent hadn't been paid, I would have been in a terrible bind. I thanked God, because things were truly in my favor.

I have a new man in my life now. Typically I'm concerned about the need for a break between relationships. Actually I've worried this time too.

GATHERING MY THOUGHTS

Perhaps the most profound lesson that I took away from my marriage was how much power words have to destroy the fiber of a relationship. Both Avery and I were emotionally and verbally abusive. I was especially harsh, my inheritance from my father. Words are powerful and lasting. Either they build or they destroy. Every putdown, insult and diminishing remark hurled at our beloved chips away at the trust, the very foundation of a loving relationship. Once callous words are unleashed, no amount of apologies, kindness or lovemaking can undo them. Your beloved may forgive you, but he will never forget. There is something about the human mind that makes it cling to putdowns while it struggles to take in praise and compliments. (It can be especially difficult for black people, who white America has historically vilified, to recover from shaming, insults and abuse.) Because of the mind's tendency to cling to the negative, we not only ought to bite our treacherous tongues when communicating with our beloved, but we owe it to them, our children, our families and ourselves to heal any inclination to resort to such annihilating words. Though too many of us allow emotional and verbal abuse to reign in our relationships, I decided to raise the bar—I would not abide receiving it or inflicting it.

I was so ashamed of how verbally abusive I had been to Avery that I vowed never again to hit a man below the belt during our times of strife. Admittedly, I have not always lived up to my pledge. More than I care to say, I've missed the mark. I, however, can sincerely tell you at last I have learned how to fight my beloved fairly; aiming for the gut is strictly prohibited. I was forced to acquire this skill. After all, I'd witnessed the devastation my words wrought on my marriage, the looks of hurt in my husband's eyes, his veiled pleas for mercy. I believe my cruel words were as much to blame for Avery's distrust of my love as my infidelity. To Avery I say, I am truly sorry for the insensitivity to your feelings and my unfaithfulness to our vows. Forgive me, please.

Love, I discovered while married, is easier said than done. Marriage is so not about the house, car or looking good together. Marriage is about commitment and communion. It's about spiritual partnership, about growing up and losing the baby fat—that is, the baggage from childhood. It's about helping your beloved grow more deeply in love with himself, as you become more authentically you through his and self-love. Marriage isn't to be taken lightly. It should be fun, but it's not a game. If you aren't prepared to be vulnerable, surrender your ego often, give generously of yourself, and heal unfinished business—then don't even think about doing it. You're not ready. You'll only hurt yourself, not to mention your beloved.

A little while ago, I sat down and re-read some of the well-written letters Avery would leave for me the mornings after we'd had a particularly tough night. In them, I could feel how deeply Avery cared for me, how much he wanted our marriage to work, and I remembered, again, what a good man

I had in this soul. In spite of his missteps and misdeeds, Avery was a dedicated family man, who adhered to the edict that a man's word was his bond. I've since met men who think nothing of breaking their commitments, which caused me to appreciate even more a man who takes his commitments to heart. Avery was that kind of man. I've since discovered that that kind of man is hard to come by.

16

TROUBLED WATERS

*The search for the perfect other is always a search for what we
sense we lack.*

MERLE SHAIN

WEDNESDAY, AUGUST 19, 1987

*I'm numb, feeling such a tremendous sense of loss. Last night,
Sterling and I decided to "just be friends." I'm newly out of my marriage, but didn't experience this frightening sense of being abandoned. Quite honestly, I had begun to feel uncomfortable about the
relationship that Sterling and I shared. I know deep down that for
my continued spiritual growth, I need a period of aloneness. I need
to learn how to feel whole without another human being in close
proximity. I'm really scared, terrified of being alone. I'm afraid of
what this means. Am I to focus on myself now, all the time? I still
want Sterling as a friend. But if having him in my life in any way
inhibits our growth as individuals, I know we must part. I'm not
prepared though. But with God in my life, I cannot only survive,
but I could soar. Please help me God, I pray.*

*I asked the question that started this ending, "Am I a plus or
minus in your life?" Sterling said he had been thinking about this
and wondering whether he should even be in a relationship with
me. Earlier, in the store, noticing that he'd brought his overnight
bag, I joked that he had the nerve to assume that he could spend the*

night with me. I really was joking but the ramifications of that joke are very serious.

A BONAFIDE WOMAN

People come into our lives to serve our highest and best good even when their presence causes us unspeakable pain. When we adjust our perceptions to see the gift in what they bring, we open ourselves to learn and grow. If we fear abandonment, that fear will draw people to us who will love us and leave us. This gives us the golden, though painful, opportunity to work on healing a belief that we could even be abandoned. A small child, wholly dependent upon others for survival, can be abandoned. A bonafide woman can be left, but she cannot be abandoned. My wounded inner child was convinced that being alone, without a man, meant certain death. Sterling blessed me with his presence—and his departure. Though our adulterous affair was wrong, he showed me attention, tenderness, care—affirming me at a time of great turmoil in my marriage and life. His presence emboldened me, lending me the strength and courage I needed to start looking forward without Avery. Then his leaving forced me to face our greatest fear—that of being alone.

Not surprisingly, women who struggle with abandonment issues invariably couple with men afraid of emotional closeness and commitment. Both people have angst about emotional intimacy. One is wired to chase. The other to run. So they dance. One advances, the other retreats. One experiences being alone as a kind of death, the other fears that togetherness would mean a loss of self, freedom and control. They tacitly agree to maintain a tolerable emotional gap between them. Since neither party is capable of relaxing into love, they have unwittingly rigged their liaison so that one partner perpetually begs—for attention, time, communication–while the other cooperates by withdrawing, avoiding, shutting down. With their beloved, they escape physical isolation yet avoid being too present in a relationship. They conveniently maintain their separate emotional spaces, while enjoying the benefits of sharing bed and bath with another. Their pact works, so long as no one upsets the applecart by demanding true emotional connection and communion. Then, all bets are off.

THE FATAL BLOW

Sterling was a bridge over troubled waters. Unwilling to wade through the rivers of life alone, I always secured a new man before leaving the one I had. Now that Sterling was there, Avery was free to go. Besides, my husband had been no angel. He had cheated on me too—once with an old flame, another time with a total stranger. Of course he blamed me. Ordinarily I would have considered it a banal cop-out for a man to blame his partner for *his* philandering. However, in this instance, I do bear *some* responsibility. In any event, my staying out all night with Sterling, something I'd never done before, dealt the fatal blow to the marriage. The fact remains, months earlier Avery and I had psychically deserted our marriage. Avery's move to another apartment merely made the separation public knowledge.

I used Sterling. He used me. People use people. The emotionally handicapped are notorious users, always enlisting others to help them get from point A to point B, frequently ditching their prey soon after. Aside from keeping a man around to guarantee that I wouldn't have the time or energy to deal with my own stuff, I used a man to prove myself a woman. A real woman, my interior and external critics contended, *has* and *keeps* a man. A lone woman was suspect—thought to be fundamentally flawed and thus undesirable. She was to be pitied.

Ironically, what really ushered in the end of Sterling and me was the collapse of our love triangle. Love triangles often thrive off the energy, and at the expense, of the betrayed partner. Add the taboo factor, the cheaters' perverse pleasure in hurting the betrayed, plus secrecy and an intense need to flee the realities of daily life, and you've got yourself a recipe for a great sex affair. As long as it was three—Sterling, Avery and me—all I saw in

Sterling was what I craved—warmth, passion and connection—all that Avery appeared to lack. But only weeks after Avery departed, my amour and I came undone. Undoubtedly, Sterling was the same man he was before Avery walked—quietly passionate, withholding, ambivalent about us. Yet now, more afraid of my neediness swallowing him whole, he pulled further away from me. Perhaps Sterling changed or perhaps he became more of himself. More than likely, it was my perception of him that changed. My perception got muddier—or clearer. In any event, this man no longer pleased me. Nor I he. I became increasingly conflicted. Though I wanted a man, my soul yearned to be free.

Our separation was brief. We weren't quite ready to let go. But with Avery went the intensity. Half-heartedly, Sterling and I limped on toward a certain death.

SATURDAY, NOVEMBER 14, 1987

I feel unloved, abandoned, lonely and alone. My love interest, Sterling, didn't answer my call nor did he call me. We barely communicate and never see each other during the week. So when the weekend arrives, I'm almost starved for hugs, touches and kisses. I wonder if I'm depending on his love too much, or if I should plan on doing without or see someone else. One problem is I don't wish to get intimately involved elsewhere.

SATURDAY, DECEMBER 26, 1987

Abrupt, distant, unromantic is the man that I spent last night with. I have to accept this and stop looking for passion, feelings and unrelenting love where it can not be found. Today I accept this with a lot more ease than I did a few weeks ago. Sterling's a friend who I sleep with. If I want romance, passion, verbal expressions of love, I'll look elsewhere. He tells me how he feels about me. His kisses and embraces are what I need to feel truly wanted and desired. I miss him. Yesterday, as I shared Christmas with him and his family, I felt so keenly the lack of closeness. He's obviously incapable of giving of himself in a way that satisfies me. Sometimes Sterling fills my world with passionate words and expressions of love. But this happens so seldom that it certainly couldn't be deemed his normal behavior.

Breaking up is often easier decided than done. Despite our challenges, there remained a genuine mutual respect and friendship between Sterling and me. All the same, I began to question why I'd gotten romantically involved with this man. Was I seeing things, or was Sterling starting to behave a whole lot like Avery—cool, remote, emotionally inaccessible? No longer finding sustenance in Sterling, fantasies of living my life without a man resurfaced. I aspired to be free, to experience the exhilaration of charting a daring course unencumbered by a man's desires or demands. I wanted to brave life all on my own, without having to answer to someone else or having to consider the impact that my decisions could have on him. I was sick and tired of acting like a child, yet my fantasies of freedom and adventure collided with the terror of the unknown, immobilizing me.

New Year's Eve, without incident, we parted. Finally we'd ceased to let our fear of flying solo keep us from heeding the call of our spirits to let go and grow.

Years later, I found myself in Sterling's shoes when I got involved with a good brother with whom I had no intentions of pursuing a commitment. He was on the rebound, and hurting deeply. I foolishly let this man use me to numb himself against the pain of a lover's rejection. Attempting to brace myself for the inevitable end of this futureless rendezvous, I asked my friend, Harvey, how does a man so easily slip away from a caring woman with not so much as a cursory glance back? Harvey explained it this way: "When a woman gets with a man on the rebound, she is nothing more than a Band-Aid to him. Just like with a Band-Aid, once the wound is all better, she is discarded." Ouch!

PAIN NOT FACED WAITS

Reaching for another person to deaden our pain, to keep loneliness at bay, or to bolster a sagging sense of self is a form of abuse that dishonors both them and us. We forget that our pain is our responsibility. Besides, addictively taking a lover only delays the inevitable—having to deal with the reality we've tried to dodge–the sting of rejection, the sadness that attends loss, the bitter anger, grief, sorrow, loneliness and fear. The day inevitably comes when we must face our demons or be destroyed by them. When we don't face our pain, it waits for us up the road. It takes up residence in our blood, cell tissue, and organs, where it implodes into cancer, hypertension, stroke, diabetes, depression, addictions. But like the body, we can heal our mind and emotions by facing our fears, feeling our feelings, and forgiving. Time alone does *not* heal. Time—plus attention to that which ails us—heals. Feeling what is there begins the journey. Don't despair. I've never met a feeling that kills. Instead, it's repression that disables and destroys us.

In light of its genesis, it was inevitable that my relationship with Sterling would quickly fizzle out. What starts out upside down seldom, if ever, ends right side up. I was a married woman. If either of us were ready for a healthy, exclusive love would we have come together under such inauspicious circumstances? Probably not.

Adding a third party to an already emotional minefield will in no way bridge the spiritual and emotional gap between two people. Yes, such arithmetic might make a bad man or marriage bearable. Yes, the taboo "extra" might fire up a cooled marital bed. As for hotter sex, it in no way translates into emotional intimacy or a richer love with your beloved—not so long as one of your affections remains divided. One must ask, "Is this the kind of love life I dreamed for myself? Why do I feel I must bear a man or marriage?" Honest answers can lead you back to your highest vision for your life.

Your belief that you're unworthy of a love of your own is what makes unavailable men appealing. A man "living" for years in an unhappy marriage isn't ready or genuinely interested in a committed loving relationship, as evidenced by his commitment to suffering. Even if he's living apart from his wife, he remains conveniently unavailable when he is still legally married. Regardless of how bad things are at home, whether or not his wife loves, understands or appreciates him, he's not available for a committed love so long as he's legally, and thus emotionally, linked to her. He is not your Prince Charming. Nor is he your Knight in Shining Armor galloping in on a white horse to rescue you from cold and lonely nights. He is but a man, a married man at that, some other woman's cheating husband. Truth is, people primed for love are *available* for love when love beckons. Love triangles are convenient escape hatches for people unable to be emotionally naked and thus vulnerable to another, people afraid to be seen and known. Such folks can be forever superficially charming with every new encounter. But when three becomes two, an adulterous affair will collapse under the weight of familiarity and real life.

It is okay to turn to another for a hand or shoulder when we lack the strength or courage to make a necessary transition alone. That's why we're here together, to be bridges over troubled waters for each other. We can, however, do so honorably, respecting ourselves and other women enough to not do so with otherwise committed men.

17

ON MY OWN

If a woman were to cast her bucket deep into the well of her own soul she would have no need for a wide net for catching a man.
THOUGHTS THAT CAME DURING MEDITATION, 10-14-01

Make your own recovery the first priority in your life.
ROBIN NORWOOD

STERLING WAS GONE. I WAS ALONE. AT THE END OF MY emotionally exhausting day helping battered women prosecute their abusers, I'd hurry straight home. I was finding God in me and I could hardly wait to see, feel, be with Her again. The more I connected with my spirit, the more I thirsted for that connection. I immersed myself in reflection, journaling, meditation, prayer, and spiritual literature. Determined to order my life from the inside out, I'd savor hours of solitude and silence. "*God help me to order my affairs,*" was my simple prayer. I so hungered for divine answers and direction. For the first time in my adult life, my love life had hit pause. I had stopped, if only for a moment, trying to append myself to a man. In my journal I wrote, "*Somewhere from within, a whole person is emerging.*" Recovery from losing my marriage and Sterling was taking place. Still, my future remained a blur of unfulfilled hopes and dreams. I needed guidance. Intuitively, I knew the answers would come from within.

How was I now going to make the fantasy of an enchanted, successful life real? It was time for a badly needed vacation. I'd recently read in a magazine article that a vacation wasn't a luxury but a spirit-renewing necessity. I took that message to heart. Now, as I struggled to live on one income, money was definitely a consideration. In no way could I afford to vacate town on my paralegal salary. So I decided to vacation at home, by the picture window in my bedroom that overlooked the beautiful Druid Hill Park. I was on a quest for answers and direction, just about any space where I could explore my interior undisturbed would do.

I revisited Shakti Gawain's insightful book, *Living in the Light*. Gawain helped me to see how my looking to a man for salvation indicated an internal spiritual imbalance. I lacked a connection with my inner male. I was out of touch with that part of me that is hard wired to take action. I looked to men to rescue, validate and support me because my inner man was fearful and weak from underutilization. I learned that it is my inner man—not the man in my life—who I am to rely upon for validation and support. It is my *inner* man's job to back me up and fulfill the desires of my heart by taking appropriate risks. Per that paradigm, I was functioning at half-mast, intuitively tuned in but afraid to back up my desires and dreams with bold action.

PROFOUNDLY DISAPPOINTED

Baffled about my tendency to get involved with insecure men with self-image issues, Gawain helped me to understand that the outer world is but a mirror image of our inner landscape. We create everything in our lives—people, places, experiences. If this is true, then I attracted "losers" because I believed I was one. If I was going to attract healthier, more self-assured winners, I had better change more than my hairstyle. My beliefs about myself, particularly those unconscious ones that lurk in the shadows, needed radical overhauling. I needed to own and embrace my competence, strength and power.

Anger consumed me. Avery had walked off. Over and over I churned the events of our lives together, dissecting, analyzing. I wanted to understand what *really* drove me to marry this man. We were incurably incompatible. I knew this from the start. I hated his weakness, detested his perpetual self-doubt, was repulsed by his façade of strength. Why couldn't he just be the man I thought he was? Why'd he have to be so damn demanding, insecure, cold, distant—so hard to love? If only he'd been different—more trusting, stronger, more emotional—then we might have made our marriage work.

Truth is, though I thought I was angry, in fact I was profoundly disappointed—with both Avery *and* myself. Anger is a mask that disappointment feels safe behind. Disappointment is what we feel when our expectations aren't met—expectations more often than not rooted in unreality. Expectations that emerge from what we think we need to be happy, not from what our beloved is capable of giving nor what our souls need to grow. Avery was supposed to be my Prince Charming and rescue me from having to devise a life worth living. Now he was long gone.

No matter the situation in which we find ourselves, we created it. I chose Avery. Yes, he was an emotional invalid—but so was I. He was but a reflection of me. What I hated about him screamed to be healed in me. It was easier though to castigate him. Fixing our attention out there, on our partner, is another trick of the ego to keep us stuck. It's only when we accept full responsibility for our circumstances that we empower ourselves to make a change. Look closely at the people populating your inner circle, then turn your energies back on you to heal what you resist and resent in them. Rest assured, if you hate something in another, it's alive and well in you. But be patient with yourself. You're a work in progress.

YOUR CLASSIC CODEPENDENT

It was Robin Norwood's *Women Who Love Too Much* that forced my relationship issues with Avery into focus. Up until that book, despite the glaring evidence, I'd dump all our marital difficulties into Avery's lap. *He* was the problem. I was caught in his tangled web. It turns out I was your classic codependent. And like every good codependent, I poured more creative energy and time into shaping, supporting and growing my man's life than I did my own. Rather than working on building my own self-esteem, I worked myself into a psychic tailspin trying to fashion Avery into the kind of man I needed him to be. It wasn't that I was incredibly loving and giving. No, that wasn't it at all. I simply fantasized that if Avery was okay, then I'd be okay. He had to live up to his potential, as I perceived it, if I were to enjoy the good life. Thus I'd expend inordinate amounts of time and energy encouraging, praising, lecturing, urging, counseling, begging, hoping, crying, and stroking my man—doing for him all the things I should have been doing for me.

Norwood was the first, and perhaps the only, person to tell me that it was not my job to make my man feel secure, capable and powerful in the world. No, that was his job. Women should, Norwood advised, focus our attention on ourselves, on our own growth and self-esteem. Now all I had to do was to embrace the empowering belief that I deserved my own attention and support.

I felt powerless in the world. Though I hardly knew it then, my desperate pursuit of the perfect man was merely my quest for a sense of wholeness and power. I would later discover that it is in our wholeness that we truly feel empowered and in charge of our lives.

WHAT THE SOUL NEEDS

At a relationship's end, bitter resentment and anger can keep two people psychically enmeshed for years. Bound together by hate, they're only dimly aware that the real target of their rage looks back at them in the mirror. Months after Avery's departure, a quiet rage tore at my peace. Daily journaling helped me to name feelings and fears. But rather than subside, for a time, the rage roared with intensity. I was angry at myself for marrying Avery. I hated that I lacked the basic skills to make love work. In any event, how was I going to carve out the remarkable life I'd envisioned for myself? With no more than a bachelor's degree in political science, how could I earn the kind of money I'd need to finance my dreams—the house, the fabulous clothes, the extensive travel? I'd tried to get into law school a year before Avery left, but was rejected. I had no plan B in place.

Mother Teresa writes, "*God is the friend of silence. Trees, flowers, grass grow in silence. See the stars, moon, and sun how they move in silence.*" Our soul, it too grows in silence. Silence tugs at our spirit, tempting us away from the noise and insanity of the world toward the peace that abides within us. I prayed for direction and the courage to heed it. I also got silent, still, and meditated. I decided to move, to take steps towards bringing more money into my life.

I wanted more than a job. I decided to enroll in a real estate course at Baltimore City Community College. I sat for and passed the required state exam, and began working as a part-time agent with Long & Foster Realtors. During that time, I met Adam on my day job.

PART THREE

GROWING PAINS

18

ANOTHER CHAPTER

You yearn for love
as the flower yearns for the sun,
and you have as much right to it.

EMMANUEL'S BOOK

I MAY HAVE BEEN PRAYING FERVENTLY FOR THE STRENGTH AND courage to chart a new course alone, however, heeding that still small voice that directed me to be still would prove difficult for a love addict. My addiction had other plans. According to my sister Ayo, in every conversation about men, I'd chant an explicit list of qualifications that my next suitor must surely show up with including—strength, ambition, power, money. Though my heart yearned for emotional health, my head pined for a man. I was torn between moving forward into the exciting unknown and falling backwards into the comfort of my familiar. I wished for something new but I had failed to plan for it. When we have no blueprint for forging a new course, we end up repeating old, addictive patterns mindlessly. Breaking destructive habits requires something of us, like putting a creative plan in place, patience and perseverance. All of which I was low on.

I met Adam October 1988, at work. He was drawn to my physical form, I to his power and position. Three days later, we went out on our first date to a pro-basketball game. We connected. Adam was married but separated from his wife for more than three years when we met. Twenty-seven days later, while Adam dressed to leave my place at the crack of dawn I lay in bed amusing him with stories about my father, the father who for the past six years had been making an apparent effort to show me a father's love. As I heard the door shut behind him, I drifted back off to sleep with fond thoughts of my dad on my mind. A few minutes later, the ringing phone woke me. It was my mother. Instinctively I knew why she'd called. It was about my father. My dad—as he drove alone from Memphis, Tennessee after attending the Church of God in Christ's annual Holy Convocation—had been in a three-car accident. He was gone.

FORGIVENESS MOVES MOUNTAINS

Six years earlier, while I was living with Ayo, one afternoon while struggling to nap in the smoldering summer heat, Spirit instructed me to write my father a letter. Obediently I put pen to paper and wrote. In the letter, I forgave my father for not loving me. I told him I appreciated the stress he must have been under, being a black man raising nine children in America. I mailed the letter to my father's Philadelphia apartment, where he lived alone. Then I went on with my life. I had no attachment whatsoever to the outcome. I don't know why, but I just didn't think to care about how or whether my father would respond. I did what I was directed to do, that was all.

I didn't realize it at the time, but this simple act of forgiveness would transform my life. God, my Higher Power, the Universe, the Creator—whatever you wish to call that intelligent, invisible force that lovingly guides our lives—is so kind and merciful. All we need do is listen and heed that still small voice that seeks to guide us toward wholeness and peace. All my life I'd wallowed in self-loathing and pain. If Daddy couldn't love me, then I was unlovable, went my internal mantra. Had *I* chose to author that letter, I would have angrily attacked, blamed and perhaps pleaded for answers. Instead, I forgave my father. This from a woman whose bitter resentment, up until that moment of grace, had effectively blinded her from seeing her father as a fallible, sensitive human being just like her. Grace handed me a new vision of my father as a man—someone with hopes, dreams, feelings, desires, regrets and failings. He was not just a father but also a person, just like me. A burden was lifted from me that day. I experienced a peace unlike any I'd ever known. Something heavy fell from my shoulders. I felt lighter, less burdened, less bound. By forgiving my father, I'd unwittingly stumbled onto the path toward freedom.

Forgiveness can be a spontaneous act or a protracted process that takes years to completely take hold. Mine was largely spontaneous but, as is often the case, it would take decades to stamp out the relics from past traumas—diminishing thoughts, self-defeating beliefs, and self-sabotaging behaviors. Forgiveness begins the journey of healing, a long, gradual process of rediscovery and recovery. Healing is about letting go of the lie that you are damaged and therefore undeserving of the best that life offers. It's about remembering the truth of who you *really* are—whole, worthy and undeniably intrinsically lovable. Not because of what you've done or have *not* done, achieved or failed at but because you are *here*. Here by divine design.

Adam arrived only weeks before my dad transitioned, to help me finish growing up. Though the two of us pretended otherwise, we intuitively knew he was not so much my lover, but my surrogate father.

My letter to my father worked its magic. Wiping the slate clean, forgiveness gave my father permission to be different with me, to show me the love he had withheld from me in my youth. We got six years. That's what came out of my obedience to Spirit—six precious years of being my father's daughter.

You may need to forgive someone who has passed away. You'll never have the opportunity to tell them how they hurt you or to hear or experience their love. But forgiveness is a gift we give ourselves. The person who hurt us need not be a part of this process. Forgiveness heals you, the forgiver. It frees you from your past, giving you a chance to start anew. I know a woman who was betrayed by people she once worked with, people she believed cared for her. Because she refuses to forgive her former co-workers, she drags her distrust and expectation of betrayal with her to every subsequent job. And just as she expects, on every job she's mistreated and isolated. Walls of resentment and fear separate us from our good, from others, and from experiencing life's beauty and bounty. When we refuse to forgive others—and ourselves, we suffer. Forgiveness alleviates that suffering. Give it to yourself, no matter the transgression.

19

IDENTITY CRISIS

I only want to reclaim myself.

NIKKI GIOVANNI

Every relationship and experience is an opportunity for you to grow and transform your life. In every one, you will have to choose how to exercise your power.

CAROLINE MYSS, *Sacred Contracts*

THURSDAY, FEBRUARY 23, 1989

Maintaining a separate identity can be a struggle for a woman in a relationship. I'm now feeling the persistent pull, tug, and war between my need for time and space for myself and the desire to be responsive to my partner's needs. Resentment toward Adam is welling up in me and I just want to run. He calls me all day and sometimes through the night. I let him know my every move. What am I doing? I feel like his prisoner. Of course he doesn't understand my feelings about this because he contacts me at his convenience. I never have time to miss, want or yearn for him, and then he wonders why I don't want to spend my evenings with him. Shucks, by that time, I'm all talked out. It's all quite painful. I want the self-back that I've allowed to semi-merge with Adam. I don't like him or me when I lose my individuality.

Men often pretend to be stronger than women but in all actuality they lean a great deal on us. His frequent calls are certainly a form of dependence. It's okay but he keeps significant parts of himself from me. Then he gets defensive when I suggest that he not interrupt my day so much. It's extremely important that men have friendships. I bet those men who do are healthier and happier. People think it's a compliment when they say they only need you to be happy. It's too much of a burden for one poor soul to bear.

PEOPLE FIT TOGETHER LIKE PUZZLES

People fit together like pieces of a puzzle. No matter how ill-matched or crooked the fit may appear to spectators, two people drawn together are meant to be. They have life lessons to learn from one another. In *A Return to Love*, Marianne Williamson writes, "*Relationships are assignments. They are part of a vast plan for our enlightenment, the Holy Spirit's blueprint by which each individual soul is led to greater awareness and expanded love. Relationships are the Holy Spirit's laboratories in which He brings together people who have the maximal opportunity for mutual growth.*"

Adam—like Sterling and Avery—hadn't showed up in my life to prop me up. Instead he had come to show me how to stop leaning emotionally on men. Adam, especially in his professional life, was capable, ambitious, tenacious, bold and fearless—all the things I believed I was not. I felt weak where I believed him to be strong. I was a damsel in distress, believing I was in dire need of being saved. Rescuing was the name of his favorite game. We were the perfect match.

Whatever it is that we believe to be our finest assets are the things that we flaunt to command what we want from others. Times haven't changed that much, men still use their titles, status, money, cars, the promise of trinkets and travel to pull a woman. For a woman, beauty is power. The more beautiful a woman is the more power she can wield over men. At twenty-one, I discovered I had a body. With my fit and beautiful thirty-one-year-old body, I reeled Adam in. Adam pimped his power, position and status. From there, a bartering arrangement blossomed.

THURSDAY, APRIL 20, 1989

It's been six months. Me and Adam have been in each other's life six months now. To celebrate, he sent me six roses—three red, three white. A gorgeous arrangement. We've been through a lot together, ups and downs. So much has happened in just six months. He's now committed to taking better care of himself. I've applied to law school. He really cares for me, and I, for him. Still I'm scared. I feel guilty because I'm not passionately in love with Adam. I love him, I'm just not sure if I'm supposed to be more in love. I know I care what happens to him. Want him to be happy. I have the utmost respect for him. I enjoy our time together. Still I think something's lacking.

20

IS IT LOVE OR IS IT TRICKIN'?

Our mental well-being is dependent on our capacity to face reality.
We can only face reality by breaking through denial.

BELL HOOKS

SO MANY RELATIONSHIPS THAT WE BRAND LOVE CONNECTIONS are little more than socially sanctioned bartering systems in which two people tacitly agree to exchange one need for another. Caroline Myss, author of the best-seller *Sacred Contracts*, gives it a familiar name—prostitution. In *When Chickenheads Come Home to Roost*, author Joan Morgan, using the street vernacular, pointedly calls it "trickin." Regardless of what it's called, when we use our minds, bodies and spirits as commodities to acquire money, power and prestige we betray our highest and best self.

Deepak Chopra sums it up this way: "When two people meet in satsang (the sharing of spirit), they can bring the fullness of their Higher Selves, yet what most of us bring to courtship is not fullness but need. When need dominates over love, the fragile thread of spirit is broken. Need implies a lack in oneself, a missing piece that someone else must supply. Women are generally asked to supply the softness, nurturing, comfort, beauty and affection that men cannot otherwise find within. Men are expected to supply the strength, protection, power and will that women cannot otherwise find. Both feel that the other has made them complete."

It may sound like a smart trade, however, you cannot prostitute one part of you, say, your body, without also trickin' your mind and spirit. I gave my body—mind and soul—to Adam for a taste of his power, emotional, financial and professional support. And for that, I would ultimately pay in self-esteem.

The ego is a cunning, constant companion, and if we're not ever vigilant it will cleverly seduce us into betraying our best selves again and again. In a conversation with my friend Stewart, I told him about my most recent triumph over my ego's attempt to lure me into a relationship with a man to which my spirit clearly shouted "NO!" Before I could finish listing the reasons my ego had for why hooking up with this new man was a splendid idea, Stewart added, "Uh huh, that's trickin." "Yes, that's tricky," I echoed. "No," he corrected. "That's *trickin*." He elaborated, "We use defense mechanisms—denial, rationalization, justification and minimization—to justify our continuing to engage in addictive, irresponsible behaviors." To this I added "and don't forget glorification, that defense mechanism that we employ to elevate lower-self behaviors to the level of respectability." In short, defense mechanisms are the myriad of clever mental devices people fashion to avoid taking full ownership of their choices.

AFRAID OF BEING ALONE

Fear of aloneness led me to repeatedly compromise myself. My failure to believe in me, in my capacity to create a life of beauty, elegance and power without a man drove me away from my highest vision for my life. Once again, my shadow beliefs were at work. I yearned for power, secretly, but feared it more. Power was something other people had, that men had, but not me.

In *Sacred Contracts*, Myss addresses the issue of power, how it intimidates people into wholesaling their power away. She lays out the four primary archetypes (patterns) of survival that exist within each of us: The Child, Victim, Prostitute and Saboteur. "*Together they represent the issues, fears, and vulnerabilities that cause us to negotiate away the power of our spirits within the physical world,*" she writes. I identify with them all. At different times in my life, different ones have taken center stage. There have been times when I have entertained them all in a single day. With Adam, prostitute and child dominated. The sheer ugliness of the word "prostitute" tempts me to disown my behavior, but I won't. I can appreciate that prostitution, just like playing the victim or self-sabotaging, is solidly rooted in fear. Fear of being powerful. Fear of wielding power. Fear of mishandling power. An overwhelming but unconscious fear of alienating those we love and cherish if we dare to embrace our most powerful selves.

Prostitution takes many forms, the least of which is the exchange of one's body for another's bounty. It's about compromising parts of ourselves—our morals, intelligence, values, integrity—in return for goods we think are beyond our ability to acquire with our integrity intact. It's going to a job that pays the mortgage but kills your spirit. It's staying in a toxic relationship that jeopardizes your very life because you're convinced that you're unable to negotiate the world without a man. Or entering into a new relationship, not for love but instead for a place to hide from life's unceasing demands. Or accepting an opportunity not right for you because you can't see anything better on the horizon. Prostituting ourselves is about letting fear rather than faith dictate our choices and decisions. Myss continues, "*The Prostitute archetype dramatically embodies and tests the power of faith. If you have faith, no one can buy you. You know that you can take care of yourself and also that the Divine is looking out for you. Without faith, however, you will eventually meet the price you cannot turn down.*"

"Faith," says the Book of Hebrews, "is the substance of things hoped for, the evidence of things seen." Fear stands opposite faith, tempting us to settle for what's before us rather than holding out for the invisible good that awaits us. While faith anchors us in our sweetest possibilities, giving us the audacity to believe in our wildest dreams, fear tempts us to relent, give in, and to give up. Faith is like a muscle, the more you use it, the stronger it gets. And use it we must, by consistently backing it up with right thinking and right action.

21

THE POWER OF DESIRE

Desire informs us of our power to co-create the future.
JALAJA BONHEIM, PH.D., *The Hunger for Ecstasy*

God's delays are not His denials.

BETH MENDE CONNY

I GOT INTO THE UNIVERSITY OF BALTIMORE SCHOOL OF LAW. AT last, my dream of becoming a lawyer was solidly in my hands. I'd secretly dreamed this dream since I was a little girl of about ten. I don't even know from whence it came. I didn't choose it. It chose me. It was a desire that wouldn't loose me—no matter what or who crossed my path. Miraculously, this desire pulled into my world all the right people and experiences that I needed to make it real. Desire. Oh what a mighty force it is in our lives, inspiring us to co-create with God our deepest soul's longings. A powerful magnetic force, desire is the God force driving our dreams, without which dreams are mere fanciful wants and wishes.

Our minds and bodies have desires. They desire to be fed, rested, moved, touched. Our heart has desires that are equally as compelling. They are born out of our soul's need to grow, God longing to be expressed in our lives through us. Here's good news—heart desires come fully equipped with everything we need to manifest them. Thus we need not figure anything out to make our dreams come true. We must, however, think enough of ourselves to listen to and passionately follow them. Chopra distills this idea down to this: "*Inherent in having the desire is the seed and mechanism for its fulfillment.*" If you don't know your heart's desires, get still. Get quiet. Meditate. Pray. Go inward. Our heart speaks to us. Listen. Now repeatedly put one foot in front of the other toward its fulfillment. Now you're on path! It's that easy.

TRUST THAT YOU ARE WORTHY

I had no idea whatsoever, after being denied admission to law school in 1986, that I'd get another stab at it. Inexplicably, gradually, over the next three years everything needed to make it happen materialized. I merely take credit for holding the vision, without which law school could not have happened. That vision of one day being a practicing attorney sent me to undergraduate school where I majored in Political Science. That vision led me to volunteer in the Sex Offense Unit of the State's Attorney's Office after graduating college, eventually leading to my being hired to work in the Domestic Violence Unit where I was surrounded by lawyers. Working in the midst of lawyers stoked my desire and resolve to become one. Our vision is the cohering energy that attracts the people and experiences that propel our life forward. Nothing great comes about without a vision. Of one thing I am certain, God enlisted Adam to help me realize my dream of becoming a lawyer. I—the one marked by her father as destined for certain failure—would become the first and, to date, only attorney in the Ricks clan. Theologian Howard Thurman tells us there are two fundamental questions that we must ask ourselves: "*Where am I going?*" and "*Who will go with me?*" He cautions us to ask these pivotal questions in the correct order—first *where*, then *who*. Where you are going takes precedence over who is or is not going with you. My intuition continually whispered the *where*, while the *who* always seems to remain an unfolding mystery. Both require trust. Trust in God. Trust in Self. Follow your heart. Trust God to handle the details.

Banish the thought that you must know how it's all going to unfold before you start—or at any point. Discard the idea that you can see the big picture, or that what you see is all there is, or can be relied upon. You won't know all of it. You're only given pieces of the dream at any given time. Rely not on your own understanding, says the Book of Proverbs. Trust God. Trust your God Self. Trust what's in your heart, what vibrates in your soul. Trust is the key to unlocking the power of God in your life. Relax and trust. Trust that the desires of your heart are within your reach, that nothing is too good or too big for you. Trust that you are worthy. Trust your heart's desires enough to protect, nurture and attend to them. And remember, whatever you are seeking is seeking you. Our destiny is branded on our souls. No one or nothing—not your mother, not your father, not your children, not your husband, not your lover, not your past—have the power to steal your destiny unless you give them that power. Don't.

22

SOUTH AFRICA

Just as you breathe in and breathe out
Sometimes you're ahead and other times behind
Sometimes you're strong and other times weak…

LAO TZU, *Tao Te Ching*

Nobody knows what I am trying to do but I do and I know when
I succeed.

GERTRUDE STEIN

SATURDAY, AUGUST 7, 1993

Sitting here in the Belson Hotel in Brussels, Belgium. Just thought I'd note that. We're in the Sabena Airport, Belgium. It's been my goal to feel comfortable anywhere in the world. Well, I'm being tested. Adam and I are headed to one of the most oppressive regimes in the world.

I feel as though I'm constantly challenged. Who I am seems to be subject to continual challenge. I must be able to look anyone in the face without buying into his or her preconceived notions of me. I am who I am. I am God's creation. No more and no less than another. Hierarchies are human constructs. And so I must decide and hold firm to the belief in my own worth and beauty.

I'm sure that comfort breeds decay. Challenge, however, encourages growth. In fact, without challenges we wither and die inside, never to truly learn who we are. I want, I must, uncover me. I owe *this to myself and God. Adam just said this trip is exciting. Scary but exciting, he said. Yes. I agree. As I meet my fears, I face myself, my true, courageous self. This is what living is supposed to feel like. I've done very little in my life of which I've not feared. Always, when it's over, I'm a bit stronger, more beautiful. I want great things to happen in my life. I want to live close to the edge. I must know more of me. And I'm acutely aware that there's only one way to self-dis-covery, it is through looking at one's fears, staring them down and refusing to be defeated by them.*

As I sit here on the floor of the Sabena Airport waiting to board a plane to the Republic of South Africa, I am reminded that life is not for the timid. It is for the brave, the courageous. I'm not brave because I fear not. I'm brave because I act despite my trepidation. I am willing. I am willing to learn.

In this moment, I feel strong. I know that I belong anywhere I choose to be. It is indeed up to me.

9:50 P.M. BELGIUM

I'm in search of a peace. It's a peace that comes from doing, from conquering. I know that there's so much to me yet to be uncovered, explored, shared. What is it that prevents me from embarking upon this seemingly inevitable journey of self-discovery? Often I think of doing more with my writing…daily, in fact. I'm such a thinker. Always exploring the why of things. I believe, on some level, that there are books in me. If not books, at least essays, articles. But if so, then where are they? Why have they not emerged onto paper? Perhaps something must happen to trigger my eventual writing. Or perhaps I must simply learn by doing, to trust that inner, knowing voice and let it speak.

I remember several years ago having an irresistible compulsion to go to the movies at least once every two weeks. I loved dramas and horror movies. I realize now that the movie going was a reflection of my need for excitement and exploration. Sitting in the dark the-ater, I could vicariously experience living life the way I imagined it should be lived.

I need the movies much less today, now that I am moving. I think all that we gravitate toward reveals us, some unfulfilled need. And as long as I was stuck in a job that did not belong to me, i.e., which did not permit me to use my talents and skills and to grow, I needed a quick fix in the dark. I wanted adventure but was afraid that I didn't deserve to live like those on the silver screen. Things have changed. They continue to change.

The more I examine the things to which I am attracted and those which I seek to avoid, the closer I get to knowing what it is that makes me pleased with my life. I'm never going to be okay with only what is familiar to me. I want more because it makes me more. Not that I become better than others, but better than the earlier me. I feel so filled. I want to know what it is like to dine with kings and queens. I want this despite the criticism that I arouse for wanting more than the ordinary. No one predicted great things for me. But I am surer every day that I am destined to leave a mark on the minds of the doubters.

When I travel, I feel a strong, irrepressible urge to take every sight, moment, experience inside me for my enlargement. I like growing, becoming. Traveling does that for me.

Now that law school is behind me, what now? I am almost tempted to hold my breath until November 12, when the bar results come out. But I know this would be wasteful, whether I pass or fail. I've not failed many things that I've pursued. That tells me, too, that I need to risk more. I am too safe. Like my job with the judge... I'm sure the fact that Adam knows him well gave me the added courage to interview with him. I'm prepared to reach further, to swim out further into unknown, uncharted waters. If I am to grow, I've got to stop asking Adam's permission and guidance. My intuition is my best guide. Well, we live and learn.

Women, including me, are often like little children. We first seek approval, then we act. I'm an adult now. It's time to act first and not feel compelled to talk about it. If I'm going to own my life, I've got to learn to do this.

The ultimate truth is self-definition. We are so outer-directed that we hardly know what we like, what we need, what we want, or who we are. Everyday I struggle. Sometimes it doesn't feel difficult because I've fallen back into the familiar but sad trap of being what I perceive others want me to be. But in my more conscious moments, especially when I travel, I'm reminded of the need to self-define. And that this unknown self is who I really am. That is when I'm happiest. Going to South Africa conjures up many self-doubts. Earlier, I was afraid to look whites in their faces for fear of what I might see. I was afraid that in their stares I might see their disdain for me. I feared that in their eyes it would be confirmed that I am indeed inferior.

Then, in the crowd at Sabena, I found a space on the floor and began to write. I wrote to myself, my little girl self, and I talked and communed with God. Both God and my core self told me to look anyway, that in the looking I must remember that hierarchies based on race and gender are human constructs. As I wrote, I could feel the fear subside. I got up with a newfound strength and determination that I would not internalize "their" negative views of me. I decided that it was me and my Creator who give/decide my value. As I moved into the crowd, boarding the plane for South Africa, I grew a little stronger, a little more beautiful.

Every time I embark upon the unknown and meet the challenge, I am reminded of my role in loosening the chains of oppression. I was no more afraid in the Sabena Airport than I was when I was the only African American in my Gender and the Law class. For several weeks I would go home and grapple with my identity. I would discuss with Adam what "self" I should be in this, what I perceived to be, threatening if not hostile environment. I discovered very early on that the history or present condition of the lives of black women was not going to be discussed. Once again I felt a responsibility to make me, us, visible. But I didn't want to take a defensive posture. I knew that I had to survive that class. I also knew I must not leave there feeling ashamed. I could not permit anxiety to rob me of the opportunity to grow, to become more of myself. So I decided to take it a class at a time. Each class I would challenge myself to be inwardly motivated. If I had something to say, I'd say it. If not, I would not talk simply to be speaking, to make a point that was pointless. With time, I began to enjoy the class and I discovered, again, that I was as smart, if not smarter, than many of "them."

I wrote a paper titled The Subordination of Black Women in America. I unabashedly discussed my history, of which I am no longer ashamed. I talked briefly about my mother's life. For the first time, I unashamedly told whoever would listen that she'd been a domestic worker. With every "coming out," that is, every time I embraced my heritage without shame, apology or the desire for understanding, I grew a little taller and moved that much closer to my true self.

I left that class whole. Neither the professor nor students nurtured me. I no longer expect those who might benefit from my pain to nurture me. But my partner, my friends, my sister and, most of all, I held my hand through another challenge. I know now, though I must constantly remember, that I am the final arbiter in my life. We live our real world from the inside out. The challenge is to project this authenticity into the world.

WEDNESDAY, AUGUST 11, 1993

Will anything worthwhile come from this trip? Adam and I had a big fight. I depend on him too much. He encourages it. There I go blaming him again.

It's hours later. My journaling was interrupted by William, the court interpreter we'd met earlier coming from the courtroom. I'm sitting in my room now; Adam has decided to sit and stare at me. I'm doing everything I can not to laugh. Moments later, I do not wish to laugh. Men. Society conditions women to lean on them, still. And when we do, they do the human thing and let us fall, sometimes flat on our faces.

I went back to the Supreme Court in Johannesburg, to see William. We talked some more about the state of the world, partic-

ularly South Africa, and had lunch. He also took me to a Democratic Party office where I met several DP workers. Finally I got an opportunity to talk with some African women. Later, back at the courthouse, I met a teacher, a court employee's wife. She believes, as do many Africans, that America is much better than Africa in terms of race relations. Yes. It is. And yet it is not. America, more so than SA, is much more image-conscious. Political correctness is the order of the day in the U.S. of A.

How does a woman attain full personhood when her own internal critic constantly admonishes that a woman mustn't do this or can't do that? I want to go into a bar for a drink. It would even be nice to meet a man for a chat. Yet I question whether this is wise, not knowing South Africa's social mores. How will I be perceived? I fear that as a black woman, I might be thought of as loose, easy. Damn social mores! But I don't mean it. I resent the double standards that restrict my movement through this world. Why must I justify or apologize for an adventurous nature? It's deemed an attribute in a man. In a woman? Well, what on earth does she intend to conquer, society demands to know. How about herself, to start?

Here I am in the hotel's bar. I'm ashamed to admit that I actually asked a waiter, a man who works in the Gazebo Restaurant, if a lone woman is negatively perceived in a bar. "No" was his answer. I'm a virtual prisoner in my own female body. Perhaps whoever said anatomy is destiny knew exactly of what he spoke. I labored something terrible over whether or not to come in here. Now that I think of it, the only women in here are African. Two African women are sitting together at a table. Before venturing in, I peeked in, wondering if they were prostitutes.

What does that say about me, and my perception of us? Well, admittedly, they looked idle, as if waiting for someone to entertain them or give them some assignment. I hate to see women out together looking past each other, as if the company they keep, with one another, isn't good enough.

I'm a product of the society in which I live. I am apt to turn my power over to the man in my life. Sure, he encourages it. He too is conditioned. On a very basic level, I resent my doing that. Adam is *about to see a new me. In a very pathetic and sick way, I seek his permission and approval for how to live.*

It may mean the demise of us. This is a chance I must take. Actually, what I want for myself is inconsistent with being in a relationship with Adam, as I currently know it. I think if a woman is to experience true personhood, she must be willing to fly in the face of both her inner critic and society's proprieties. Who, anyway, determines what is or is not proper? If I didn't have a hand in designing the rules, why then should I have to adhere to them?

FRIDAY, AUGUST 13, 1993

We're back in Brussels, headed to Paris, France. I'm feeling a little sad. Not sure why. I think the next trip I take I'll take alone. It's time for me to grow up. Another thing, on the next trip I plan to travel much lighter. We have too many bags. Bags cut into the enjoyment of the trip.

FRIDAY, AUGUST 13, 1993, PARIS, FRANCE

I'm sad knowing I need to drift away from Adam. Our relationship is out of balance. No, I do not want a bossy, chauvinistic man, but I do need a strong man. Adam is strong in many ways, except with me. In our relationship he's basically a wimp. For example, yesterday we were looking for a place to eat. I suggested a restaurant. We stopped in the doorway of one. I decided I wanted an outside table, but none were available. In mid-step, Adam backed up with this horrible frown on his face. As we walked up the street, in search of another restaurant, I asked him what was wrong. "Nothing" he lied. Finally, after much to do about nothing, he confessed that he had been ready to eat at the restaurant that we just left. I suspected, given the scowl on his face, that all was not well. But rather than expressing his desires, Adam caved in to what I wanted. Where are his wants and needs? I'm tired of trying to teach this man how to be selfish enough to stay interesting. It's getting harder and harder to suppress my need for interaction with another individual, someone who isn't merely a reflection of me.

That's what Adam does. He responds to me. I want to be with someone who has real interests, who is committed to his own growth and self-development. Selfishness has its place. Self-sacrificing people burden me. They bore me. I like getting a man to do things and see things my way, with a bit of a struggle. This relationship is lopsided. He lets me take and take, never pulling far enough away for me to have to reach for him, to chase, to go after him—because he never leaves. He clings. He has tried to change this. I suppose he has done his best. Well, I guess we are at the end of our journey. It saddens me to know this. We are better friends than lovers anyway.

23

LIVING UNCONSCIOUSLY

When a woman falls in love with the magnificent possibilities within herself, the forces that would limit those possibilities hold less and less sway over her.

MARIANNE WILLIAMSON, *A Woman's Worth*

I NEVER DREAMED I'D SET FOOT IN NELSON MANDELA'S SOUTH Africa. Before apartheid toppled, the mere mention of the word "apartheid" in the news stopped me in my tracks. The idea of actually bearing witness, with my very own senses, to one of the most oppressive regimes in the universe both frightened and fascinated me.

We had accommodations at the Sandton, an upscale hotel and mall complex in the city of Johannesburg where the housekeepers, all black women, scrubbed stubborn stains from the rooms' carpeted floors on their hands and knees. This trip was poignant in many ways, one of which has little to do with where I was physically but everything to do with where I was emotionally and spiritually. Wedged between vivid memories of a middle-aged white saleswoman, face distorted by fear and confusion, chasing me around a highbrow boutique pleading, "*Can I help you? Can I please help you?*" are recollections of signs of the vast difference in the standard of living for blacks and whites and the arrogance and blatant racist attitudes of some of the fearful whites as the dismantling of apartheid became more real to them. There I was in one of the most intriguing countries in the world and yet the most riveting experience that I had was largely about me.

Our stay in South Africa was during the month of August. One of Adam's clients financed the trip, made all the flight arrangements, booked the hotel, and even planned the itinerary. It was business for Adam. For me, an opportunity to experience what felt like another world. I delayed starting my judicial clerkship with a circuit court judge, packed too many bags, and cheerfully accompanied Adam on three planes en route to the Republic of South Africa. Arriving in Johannesburg in the black of the morning, we took a taxi to our hotel on the outskirts of the city. I was amazed to see how familiar Johannesburg looked, just like any big American metropolis at night, towering, ultra modern structures decorated the skyline. Upon arriving at our room, exhausted, I happily retired for the morning, anticipating the thrill of waking up in a new place, with new people, new possibilities. Hours later I bounded from bed, showered and dressed—eager to lay my eyes on South Africa in the flesh.

I stepped outside into chilled, brisk air, and my excitement quickly dissolved into fury. It was wintry, not summery. I wore a pair of summer pants, a cotton blouse, and open toe shoes, however, it was cold outdoors. Smiling, the bellhop remarked, "It is winter." I was pissed and embarrassed. Guess who I blamed? I tore at Adam, blasting him for failing to tell me what time of year it was in this part of the world. I had no money to buy warmer clothing, so I demanded that he buy me some. What I got was a sweater and a shawl. My trip was ruined. Seven days ahead of me in this fascinating country with little to nothing to wear, a woman's worst nightmare.

Let's be clear. Nobody else is going to have our best interest at heart. That's our job. Everybody's basically looking out for themselves, for their needs, their wants. If we don't see that our needs are met, it's unrealistic to expect that they will be. It's nobody else's responsibility to provide for us. That too is our charge. There I was, almost a member of the bar, expected to make decisions on behalf of others. But still, at thirty six, I had yet to assume responsibility for every aspect of my own life. That's so common of women. We volunteer to save the planet but let our own lives unravel around us. That's unconscious living at its height. We don blinders when we feel ill equipped to take care of ourselves. It's yet another way our hidden beliefs drive our life. We hope and pray that things will somehow work themselves out, without our help.

MAMA SAID JESUS WILL FIX IT

A couple of years ago, with my sister Ayo I co-facilitated a six-week support group for women living in a transitional house. This experience helped me to see how unconscious living can be a learned behavior that ultimately derails life plans when it goes unchecked. We asked the participants to return to their childhood for beliefs, attitudes and behaviors that might be contributing to their homelessness. Joyce—a bouncy, good-natured forty-something year old woman—refused to venture far from her perception of her childhood as healthy and happy. She maintained that her God-fearing adoptive mother had given her a warm, culturally rich life brimming with love and security.

As with most of the exercises, Joyce drew a blank. Staring up at the light fixtures, I could see her surfing her mind for a fitting response. Nothing. "The only thing I can remember," she started, as her right hand slowly found her chin where it began to mimic plucking motions, "was my mother picking her face and telling me, 'Don't worry baby, God will f-i-xxxx it.'" The light in Joyce's eyes brightened as she made the connection, for the first time, between her mother's passivity and her homelessness. "But," Joyce continued, "the gas and electric was off, bill collectors were calling, and mother would just sit there plucking her face!" Joyce realized that the reason she and her five children were homeless was not because she wasn't a capable woman. It was due, in part, to learning to deny her reality whenever she felt overwhelmed by it.

We tend to choose unconsciousness when we fear we are ill-equipped to handle the challenges that life invariably serves up. I've found one thing that works, something that Debbie Ford, author of *The Right Questions*, talks about. If I live from my humanity, I can only see so far ahead of me. Because I have no idea from where the money, say, for a bill is coming, I avoid answering the bill collectors' calls. But when I choose to live from my divinity, I suddenly have access to a reservoir of strength and courage that empowers me not only to face my reality, but miraculously, to also fix the problem.

Life is hard. It will challenge you. Life will present you with situations that look unsolvable. Just when you think you've gained some mastery over life, it will throw you a hard curve ball. It's a trick of the enemy—and our friend—called fear. There is no mountain that you can't successfully scale when you're equipped with the right attitude and tools.

I was reared to believe in an old white bearded man that dwells in the clouds. This God was mean, temperamental and punitive when pissed off. He would, they said, only love me when I behaved well. But if I missed the mark by behaving "badly," this God would punish then abandon me. This God, they said, is everywhere except inside of me. Nonetheless, I was encouraged to blindly wait and rely upon this God.

I have since found God for myself. This God that I have found loves me. This God dwells within me. And when I feel really bold, I *am* god. Not the ALL Intelligence ALL Knowing God, but a little "g" god. Whenever I slip back into relating passively with God, I suffer. I suffer immensely. Then, I believe, God gets pissed off with me. Why? Because God doesn't want us to see ourselves as helpless little cods that must sit idly by hoping, praying and waiting for what we ought to be doing for ourselves. No, we are to act as co-creators with God. When we remember that God abides within each of us, that She/He/It is our Higher Self, we are able to live empowered, abundant lives on purpose.

24

MARCH FORTH

If you are constantly being mistreated, you're cooperating with the treatment.

DR. ROBERT ANTHONY

Any man who holds a woman back is not a man a woman can afford to be with.

MARIANNE WILLIAMSON

FRIDAY, MARCH 4, 1994

I guess it's about time I experience being without male companionship. All my life I've believed I had to have a man. Though I was progressing educationally and spiritually, it took three decades for me to know emotionally that I do not need a man to be complete. Finally. In fact, I rather enjoy two things…being alone and being in the company of my sisterfriends. They are far more interesting company. Women know better how to self-disclose. And they see the gray areas.

Inside of me is a woman waiting to be discovered and rediscovered. Men. I have looked to them for missing parts and pieces of myself. They leave me wanting—since it isn't them but me that I want! I want to find me, explore me, know me, experience me, enjoy me.

Life is full of all sorts of strange and seemingly coincidental happenings. Yesterday while shopping at my new Macy's, Value Village thrift store, I ran across the Cinderella Complex by Colette Dowling. How telling. I'm only on Chapter 1 and I see me on every page. It's frightening. Not really, it's delightful. Dowling talks about women's fear of independence, our belief that someone someday will rescue us. So we're always playing the waiting game, failing to do the necessary things to make our lives truly full and free. Meanwhile stifling our creativity, burying it beneath busy work, inertia and caretaking— caring for everybody but ourselves.

TAP THE POWER WITHIN

I could no longer endure the lies, deception, womanizing and increasing hollowness of my relationship with Adam. I was suffering horribly. The pretension and shame was killing my spirit. I had to leave him.

Why had I put up with this anyway? Was I still afraid of being alone? Probably. However, I knew continuing in a relationship where I was disrespected and dishonored was no longer acceptable. So I told Adam, "It's over." That was January 1994, right before I sat for the Maryland bar exam, for the second time.

Among battered women's advocates, there has been a tacit agreement among the leadership to insist upon seeing and thus labeling battered women as victims. Hence, many may consider what I say here as sacrilegious. As I've noted earlier, I don't believe in victimhood, though I realize a woman can certainly be *victimized.* During my years as a battered woman's advocate and attorney, I purposely avoided referring to my clients as victims, knowing to do so would be tantamount to concluding that their circumstances defined them and that they were powerless to change them. Whenever a new client came to me, along with the legal information and advice, I provided them with a healthy stream of you-have-the-power-to-take-charge-of-your-life counseling. Woman after woman responded positively, for though they appreciated the usefulness of a protective order, they were also clear that their real work was spiritual, even if they opted not to do it. These smart, brave women intuitively understood, before I opened my mouth, that we teach people how to treat us.

No matter the abuse a woman tolerated in her intimate relationships—physical, emotional, psychological, economic—there was one constant weaving its way through every situation, the woman was terrified of being alone and of assuming full responsibility for her own life. Giving her life over to her abuser was an attempt to escape the hard work of managing the life God gifted her. Abuse was the price she agreed to pay to be "taken care of." I understood these women because I walked in their shoes, permitting all manner of emotional and psychological abuse. Like them, I'd decided that cruelty and violence was more bearable than having to negotiate life on my own without a man.

As every relationship is a learning experience, so are those encounters we enjoy or endure at work. One former client, 55 year-old Gwendolyn, came to me seeking an order of protection from her husband six months shy of their thirtieth wedding anniversary. Gwen, as were many of my battered clients, was severely depressed and thus on Paxil. Standing at five feet and weighing 115 lbs., Gwendolyn suffered from heart disease and diabetes. Her doctor concluded that the cause was partly stress, and so she was further medicated. I immediately liked this soft-spoken, fragile woman who appeared considerably older than her age. She shared that she and her husband had raised three children together, and now she wanted out. She was certain that if she stayed he will kill her.

Gwendolyn had good reason to believe him, since for nearly all of their thirty years of marriage Russell had brutalized her. He had punched, slapped, kicked, stomped and threatened her at gunpoint. In the most recent incident, at gunpoint Gwendolyn's abuser woke her from her sleep, forced her to undress, vowing to kill her. In terror, she bolted naked from their Northwest Baltimore home into the frigid night, stumbling, falling and crying out for help. Her neighbor of twenty years peered out from behind his blinds, then turned and walked away, leaving Gwendolyn huddling behind a bush for safety and shelter. Gwendolyn's grown son alerted the police. Russell was taken into police custody, then released on bail the following day undaunted. Gwendolyn was transported to Sinai Hospital where she was treated for two busted knees.

If you've never been physically battered, you might not appreciate that Gwendolyn's deepest wounds came not from the blows to her face but from her husband's emotional assaults and indifference. One Saturday morning, she was having severe chest pain. She pleaded with Russell to drive her to the hospital. "No", he angrily snapped, "I've got to wash my car! You can walk to the hospital. I'll come up there later." Gwendolyn sat in my office trembling, tears cascading down her brown cheeks, trying to understand how the man she'd given "the best years of her life to" could treat her so callously when she most needed his loving care.

DEALS WITH THE DEVIL

Gwendolyn did what so many women do. She made a deal with the devil then expected something holy to come out of it. Her part of the deal? To bear and raise their children, to make their home a haven, to love, believe in and support her man. Caring for herself was not a part of the agreement: she believed that was Russell's job as a husband. He was to love, cherish, protect and provide for her. Believing that she had fulfilled her part of the covenant, Gwendolyn felt cheated and betrayed by Russell.

In Hollywood's rendition of author Terry McMillan's *Waiting to Exhale*, Bernadine's husband left their eleven year marriage for his young white secretary. In a conversation with her sisterfriend Savannah, struggling to understand what went wrong, Bernadine whispers, "*You know what, it's funny. I always thought if I gave him what he needed, he'd give me what I needed. Huh, it's amazing what can happen when you give a man control over your life. I can't even pretend it's all John's fault.*" I cherish this scene because I believe it speaks to the lives of women the world over. Bernadine was awakening. Like Gwendolyn, like me, perhaps like you, she began to see the danger in placing her life in the hands of a man, any man, good or bad. Some part of Bernadine wanted to lay the blame at John's feet for losing herself, but in good conscience she could not.

Collette Dowling observes in *The Cinderella Complex*: "Once a man is on hand, a woman tends to stop believing in her own beliefs." Gwendolyn had betrayed herself. Bernadine had ceased to believe in her own dreams. I had compromised my own values to be half of a couple. What about you? How have you given your power to someone else?

Gwendolyn—who had once left Russell for six months but returned—didn't look back this time but instead forged ahead solo. Neither her daughter's clear disapproval, nor Russell's withholding financial support in defiance of a court order, nor her fragile health kept Gwendolyn from moving forward on her own. Finally she chose life over death, spiritual freedom over economic security, herself over her man. Gwendolyn is proof that it is never too late to let self-love inform our choices and to start anew.

LEAVING ADAM

Stepping into the unknown isn't easy. Frankly, it's downright terrifying. I liken it to walking through your home into a familiar but dark room. Though you have been in that room a thousand times, fear still rises up in your chest at the very thought of what could be lurking there, ready to pounce. The mind plays tricks on us, insisting that in every dark space in our life, ugly, horrible things await us, things way beyond our capacity to handle. So we stay put. Most of our energy, rather than fueling our dreams, is then used in avoiding the dark, the unknown. We only do the things we know we can do, go places we've been before, interact with people who look like us, get into relationships with people beneath us, settle for jobs that don't challenge us. We play it safe, allowing fear to cheat us out of the very things for which our heart and souls long.

I've learned that the only sure thing when walking into the unknown is to trust in my higher self, in my divinity. It helps to remember how I weathered earlier storms, similar situations that, from all appearances, came to do me in but failed.

Leaving Adam was harder on me than the dissolution of my marriage. It got even tougher after March eleventh. That day, at a sonogram ordered by my physician who suspected that he'd detected fibroid tumors during a routine pelvic exam, I got the thrilling—but shocking—news that I was going to be a mother. I was three months pregnant with Adam's baby. Was God trying to tell me something, I wondered? Was I destined to be with Adam? Though Adam and me were officially over in January, I hoped it wasn't too late to try again. I really wanted my baby to have the thing I most sought growing up—a father's love.

Couples therapy was a last ditch effort to save what I considered my unborn child's future.

25

PSYCHO ANALYZED

All emotions, even those that are suppressed, have physical effects. Unexpressed emotions tend to "stay" in the body like small ticking bombs—they are illnesses in incubation.

CHRISTIANE NORTHRUP, MD,
Women's Bodies, Women's Wisdom

The psychotherapist can only be of good to the extent he is a fellow pilgrim.

DR. SHELDON KOPP,
If You See the Buddha on the Road, Kill Him

WEDNESDAY, JULY 27, 1994

I've just had one of the worst experiences of my adult life. Adam and I attended therapy tonight. I recommended the therapist. Thought she would suit our needs. I was wrong, though I'm still examining what just transpired.

I went to her because from the little that I'd seen and read about her, I thought she could be fair, objective. Boy was I wrong, wrong, wrong. From the moment I met her, a week ago for the first time, I sensed something disturbing about the way she chose to deal with me. Significantly, she never once called my name. This may seem petty, but really it's a sign or show of respect and recognition to call a person by her name. It was downhill from there, though I was reluctant to make too much of any one thing.

Tonight, however, really hurt. I'm clear that therapy—that is, the excavation of pain—will be agonizing, at least at times. Much of the pain that I was feeling arose from this woman's persistent siding with Adam against me. Over and over again, I tried to rise above these things, to give her and the situation the benefit of the doubt. She apparently underestimated my discerning eye. It was abundantly clear by the end of the session that I was not in a safe healing space. My emotional needs were not only ignored, but at times I felt blatantly assaulted. She seemed bent on bolstering Adam's ego, while dumping on me.

We were supposed to spend tonight discussing our respective families of origin. Adam spent 80% of the too-short hour talking glowingly about his family. From where I sat, it seemed that he was clearly not in touch with reality. I mean, all of his shortcomings became adorable, tolerable little tics that ultimately made him a hero. When it came time for me to talk, he and she interrupted with more discussions about him! Where was my time?! The entire time that Adam talked, I sat patiently listening. When I shared, the conversation went back to him. And since he's so damn interesting to her, he is free to go see her, alone without me. I want no parts of therapy with this woman. She apparently has unresolved issues of her own and can't nurture another black woman, at least not this one, while a man is present. Or she just sides with the partner who pays her bill. Well, they are free to have each other, because it hurts way too much to be a part of a trio where my so-called man sides with another against me.

The therapist told me that I had self-esteem problems. Then she went on and on about some client of hers who denied having a self-esteem problem because she claims, "I'm successful." Well, I could deal with her pointing this fact out to me if it were not one of many of her attacks. See, I can handle criticism when I know it's given out of a desire to help me. No, it's never easy. Criticism stings no matter the objective. But this woman could hardly wait to leap on me while she went to Adam's aid at every twist and turn. What brings tears to my eyes even now is when Adam realized she was nurturing him but attacking and undermining me, he began—once again—to pontificate on his many imaginary virtues. With his head dropped, he began to tell her how he tries so-o-o hard to make me feel good when we're out! Finally I told them I was not interested in the old martyr story of how good he is. He has, on more than several occasions, outright disrespected me. He continued his sad saga after she, glaring at me, hollered, "This man can't be responsible for YOU!" The woman may be knowledgeable but she certainly isn't very smart. A smart therapist wouldn't assume that she was so powerful, so able to dis' the woman of a couple, and expect her to continue as a client. Perhaps she wanted me to quit. Well, the woman got what she wanted.

Then she commanded Adam to "STOP trying to help her with her stuff!" Wrong! He was not, at least not tonight, trying to help me with anything! She made me out to be a basket case. That hurts and angers me. I cried all the way home, alone. Alone because Adam never said one concerned word to me. Then when I got home, he reached over to embrace me. I refused it. Why should I hug a man who so readily abandons me emotionally because a "therapist" said to do so?

I can't sleep for crying. It's about 5:15 a.m. I awoke to pee when upon my return to bed, the pain of last night came rushing back, and the tears started to flow again. Now I can't seem to stop them.

I feel wounded, so utterly attacked and left to die. It really hurts deeply that the Adam I once knew would have cared enough to try and comfort me when I cried. Now he just ignores my suffering.

These tears are burning hot with pain. I feel ashamed to have revealed my pain in the company of two uncaring souls. As I lay here, trying to get back to sleep, my mind likens last night's experience to being put to sail in a dinky without direction or paddles. If this is good therapy, I'm not so sure I can or am willing to try to handle it.

Six-thirty a.m. feels like a long way off. Sleep doesn't seem the appropriate balm for my pain. I want it to be better real bad. I need to do a reality check with a woman friend, someone who cares for me. We can't heal in a hostile space and that's exactly what I was in last night.

SATURDAY, JULY 30, 1994, SINAI HOSPITAL

I guess the stress of the experience with that therapist woman caught up with me, stretching me out prostrate in this hospital bed.

Thursday about 4 p.m., the ulcer pains I experienced about two years prior returned with a vengeance. Again, I thought little of them, figuring with time they would ease up and go away of their own accord. I was wrong.

Judge Brown's secretary, Amanda, just left. The judge had already gone. I sprawled out on the judge's sofa in search of relief— before I would attempt to walk the several blocks to my car near Camden Yards. The razor sharp pains in my upper abdomen grew worse. Still I refused to call anyone. I could handle it alone, I thought. I'd already begun to feel like I whined way too much about my pregnancy. As God would have it, the phone rang about 6 p.m. Eddie Harrison was calling to find out if I'd gotten the fax that he'd sent the judge. Barely able to talk, I assured him that the judge would get it. Eddie wanted to know if I was experiencing any problems in my pregnancy. Bingo, just the question I needed to hear. "Yes, as we speak," I moaned. He said sweetly, "What's wrong, baby?" I told him. "I'll be there in five minutes!" he quickly said. The plan was that Eddie would drive me to my car. As I waddled to his car, my senses returned. "Take me home," I pleaded. My car could wait.

SUNDAY, JULY 31, 1994

Relationships are very difficult to sustain. Ours is no different. I'm in the hospital now because last Wednesday night I went to bed sobbing, feeling betrayed by Adam. I hardly slept four hours. I awoke at 5 a.m. to pee. I ended up crying again; I couldn't return to sleep. Work was stressful because Adam and I were constantly on the phone, arguing about the night before. He just refuses to see the significance of what transpired between him, the therapist and me. Even with some distance on the situation, it's clear that that woman has some serious problems with sisters.

Anyway, finally I'm recovering from that traumatic experience. I think the ulcer, which I conveniently forgot I had, put me in the hospital. It was wishful thinking on my part that it had disappeared. I'm just extremely pleased that the chaos in my stomach wasn't contractions. At twenty-seven weeks of pregnancy, with about eight to ten more to go, I'm not ready to bring my baby into this world. Nor is she prepared. Thank God Almighty, He wasn't ready for little Adam or DeBora to come just yet. Though my pain was beyond words, I can take it as long as my baby isn't harmed. Already, I love my baby very much.

MONDAY, AUGUST 1, 1994

So, I definitely have an ulcer. Well, it's not news to me really. I stayed home from work again today. Emotionally, I just wasn't ready to go back. I'm very glad that my judicial clerkship ends September 7th. I need a break from it all. I've worked all my life, pretty much nonstop. Many of those years I both worked and attended college or law school. I'm due not only for a break but a change. Being a mommy will not be easy, but it certainly will be different from anything else that I've ever done.

PREGANT, FAT AND UGLY

I reconsidered Adam and me. Maybe he *was* my destiny. After all, I'd left him only to discover I was having his baby, my miracle baby. (I was sure the infamous Dalkon shield IUD had ruined my chances of ever conceiving.) Adam seemed pleased, largely for all the wrong reasons. Now he had the upper hand, the power, the ultimate control since I was now pregnant, fat and ugly. Pregnancy robbed me of my one true thing, a shapely body. I'd never felt more powerless than I did during my last trimester, when I ballooned up to 175 pounds. It wasn't the interest of other men that I missed. It was Adam's. He grew cold, arrogant and aloof; at a time when I most needed his warmth and attention. It was all over his countenance. He relished my vulnerability, seizing every single opportunity to invalidate me. I was hurt and saddened by what I saw—a mean, nasty, ruthless side of this man that I didn't even know existed.

Having a baby was nothing like I imagined it would be. Essentially I was alone. Adam used that time to retaliate for the wrongs—some real, many imagined—that I'd inflicted upon him in the past. I had no man to rub my burgeoning belly and excitedly search for the baby's first kicks. I had nobody to hold my hand through gestational diabetes, carpel tunnel, the inevitable doubt that accompanies becoming a parent. There was nobody to run out to buy foods "the baby" craved. Nobody to spoon me in the dark and haggle with me over an endless list of baby names. Going through a pregnancy alone was not supposed to be a part of my becoming a mother movie. Yet this was my reality. I was with child and alone.

I desperately needed to end my connection to Adam. The time had come—and gone—for us. Yet I resisted moving on. My spirit screamed, "Go." My addiction shouted, "No!" We can choose to learn and grow through ease and pleasure or via pain and struggle. Clearly I was choosing the latter. I was terrified. There I was having this man's baby only to witness the emotional divide between us balloon out of my control. A control I never had.

Our ship was sinking, and all I knew to do was to cling tighter. Despite all the work that I'd done to grow toward emotional self-sufficiency, the prospect of bringing a child into the world alone catapulted me backward to emotional infancy. I wanted for my baby what I didn't have—a loving, involved father. I needed a co-parent, a psychological and emotional partner to help ensure that my child would get all she or he needed to develop into a super human being. I worried. And my health took a beating. If emotional pain is information, then my body was wildly flailing its arms, thrashing about, screaming, "Let go! Save *yourself!*" My body bellowed, "Let go of this toxic relationship NOW!"

TIME TO CULTIVATE SELF -VALIDATION

Therapy was an emotionally searing experience. In our second and last session, badly burned, I bolted from the therapist's office in tears. I'd do therapy again. But next time alone. And with a therapist who's in therapy herself. Titles, degrees and certificates do not a good therapist make. In therapy we're so unmasked, so vulnerable. Much greater care ought to be exercised than I had used in choosing this therapist from hell.

That was one of the most unloving, hostile spaces in which I've ever bared my soul. Thankfully, more than seven years of Adult Children of Alcoholics meetings, and the morning after reality check that I sobbed through with my therapist friend Brenda, confirmed what I intuitively knew—this therapist had a whole lot of healing to do herself. She did far more damage than good. And to think, she got paid to do it. Upon getting a bit of distance on the nightmare, one lesson for me was never to believe the hype, but to investigate and interview several potential therapists before I decide which one is worthy of my trust and time.

But it was a prenatal visit that sealed our fate as a couple, and woke me up to how I was colluding with Adam in my diminishment. In the waiting room, sitting across from me, Adam chatted with an attractive woman he knew. I sat feeling ugly and invisible, stubbornly committed to reading the magazine in my hands. I couldn't. The hurt welling up in my chest distracted me. I felt so alone, invalid and ashamed at myself for giving Adam the power to decide how I felt about me. In a flash, it hit me. I don't have to be at Adam's mercy, or any man's for that matter. No one has the power to decide the measure of my worth, nobody but me. I could—I realized—take back my power. It was I who invalidated me. That was a defining moment in my struggle for self-recovery. I vowed to never again look to a man for validation. I would validate myself.

In August of 1994, I unceremoniously ended my relationship with Adam. I was seven months pregnant and more than fed up with the crumbs he'd been meting out to me. Nothing special happened through the night. I simply awoke this sunny morning with not a shred of doubt anywhere in my being in my ability to make it on my own, without Adam. A quiet strength and deep resolve overcame me, and displaced every molecule of fear and uncertainty. Over the phone I told him, "It's over between us." Full of himself he asked, "You sure this is what you want?" "Yes," I calmly responded. "Well, you n-e-v-e-r know what the future will hold," came his reply, full self-possession and haughtiness. Finally my whole being knew that even an uncertain, frightening future as an unemployed single mother was better than the hostility and indifference I was enduring to have this facsimile of a relationship.

26

SINS OF THE FATHER

Loss can dwell within us all our life.

JUDITH VIORST, *Necessary Losses*

TUESDAY, MARCH 14, 1995

I'm not sure when I imagined it happened. However, I'd begun to believe that because I was no longer angry at Daddy, no longer in excruciating psychic pain, this meant I'd completely healed from my past. Now I see I was wrong. Had I been well, I wouldn't have chosen Adam. He was perfect for my unhealed heart. He was very unavailable, a workaholic, married even though separated. I didn't really love him. At least I was not in love with him.

So what did Adam represent for me? When I met him, I was still looking for a father. Finally I'd found a daddy who believed in me, in my dreams. Still he didn't know how to love. It took me nearly six years to no longer need the sickness, to discover that I am worthy of love, that I do deserve to be loved, that I do deserve loyalty, honesty, integrity. That I am good enough. To be quite honest, because I'm no longer in an intimate relationship with a man, I don't really know if I am healed. Yet, the fact that I didn't need another man to let go of Adam is a sign of growth for me. It's also a sign of self-love that I am taking better care of me these days.

Honestly, when I think of Adam, how fraudulent, deceptive, duplicitous he was, I shudder at the thought of having spent more than five years of my life with him. Then I remind myself that that relationship had to happen. It aided in my growth. Now that I know better, I'll do better. Problem is now that I believe I deserve a man with integrity, capable of honesty—where will I find him?

I guess the bottom line is this—just because I forgave Daddy for the sins he committed against me doesn't mean I don't continue to pay dearly for them. The Twelve-Step programs have made a tremendous difference—but I can still use some assistance in uncovering the deep-seated, nearly imperceptible pain that still acts out in my relationships with men, and undoubtedly in other areas of my life.

I'm still trying to articulate this quiet rage that I sometimes feel toward Adam. It angers me that he played me for a fool. That he pretended to be about spiritual growth, truth and honesty. To this day, I don't know what part of him was real and what part was fake.

TUESDAY, OCTOBER 1, 1996

Waiting. I've spent the greater part of my life waiting. Waiting on a man to come into my life to make me happy, to fulfill my needs—as I have defined them. Even when I've looked busy, occupied, satisfied—many times I was still in waiting. I am no longer waiting to live.

Still I've not learned how to be both centered and in love—or whether it is even possible. When I am with a man, I tend to put more into us than I do into me. Perhaps that is not so in a holy relationship, that is, in a relationship sanctioned by God. But in an unholy, going nowhere relationship, I lose myself and lose God in the process. Today I know to practice putting God in my relationship. To tell you the truth, if God isn't there, neither should I be.

GATHERING MY THOUGHTS

Every man I coupled with came to help me see into me. My soul, in its desire to grow, pulled Adam into my life to help me see that more of my wounds begged to be healed. To my life Adam brought many and varied gifts, many of which continue to bless my life today, like my daughter. I grew up with Adam. I can almost recall the instant when I went from feeling like a little girl who needed the protection and provision of a father to embracing my womanhood and all that that entails. My taste in men immediately evolved, I was no longer attracted to father figures. Suddenly I desired a man who I could partner with, befriend and love passionately as an equal.

Adam took care of me, in so many ways. He needed someone to rescue and I needed to be rescued, or so we believed. From the outset, I intuitively knew Adam was my father. Interestingly, we met just weeks before my dad would be killed in a car accident. I saw Adam later that day, before I left for my father's home in Philadelphia with my siblings. His embrace was that of a father, not a lover's. The course and tone of our relationship was set by those brief moments. We both knew, I think, why we'd come together though we never discussed it. It was an uncomfortable fit, feeling strangely incestuous.

I very much wanted to have Adam in my life, but on different terms. I needed his strength, his encouragement, his lavish emotional support. But I hated who I'd become to be with him. I knew I was prostituting myself, compromising my highest values to get my perceived needs met. Still, I did it anyway. I paid a high price for what I did, because for as long as I compromised myself to be with this man, any man, peace would elude me. And that sense of being whole and complete unto myself, well, that also remained just beyond my grasp.

I didn't enjoy my sexuality with Adam—I exploited it. My relationship with Adam showed me just how low I would stoop to avoid taking full responsibility for my own life. I not only compromised my morals and dignity, I chose to settle for an arrangement based on need rather than seek for true love based on a mind, body and spirit connection. All the while I longed to be with a man with whom there was an abiding spiritual connection. I felt cheated. And fraudulent. I understood that I was hurting both Adam and me by staying.

One of the most pivotal lessons that I learned with Adam is this—no matter how scary the future looks I have within me everything I need to successfully negotiate it. As I lay in the hospital bed in the dark the day I was to take my baby home, I prayed for the strength and courage that I would need to go it alone as a new mom. Adam had broken his promise to take time off from work to help with our new baby. God sent an angel, a nurse who talked to me. Within, I found strength I'd forgotten about. With a brand new resolve, I called on my friends—Ernesta, Chance and Liz. They looked after me and my baby—cooked, washed, shopped—until I was able to negotiate the stairs again. The nurse helped me to remember my power to create, reminding me that I wasn't powerless simply because one person withheld his support from me. If my baby's daddy wasn't there for us, it didn't have to mean I was without support. No, I had a support system. My baby and me were not alone. We are never alone. Support is always available. We need only reach for it. When we do, who and what we need will miraculously appear.

With Adam, I saw how pathetic a woman is when she looks to a man to give her life meaning and value. A man can invalidate you only to the extent that you depend on him for validation. An empowered woman validates herself. The power Adam used to invalidate me was power I gave him. Since I'd been the one to giveth, then it follows that I had the power to taketh back.

PART FOUR

FINDING MY WAY

27

DIVINE DISCONTENT

*I have never
been contained
except I
made
the prison.*

MARI EVANS

*My true relationship is my relationship with myself—all others are
simply mirrors of it.*

SHAKTI GAWAIN

TUESDAY, FEBRUARY 10, 1998

*I want so badly to be my own boss. Working for others is no
longer okay. Perhaps this is what this job is teaching me—that I
need to step out on my own. I feel the pull toward self-employment
most strongly when a supervisor treats me like a child, like I was
treated today. Some of her behavior was warranted—but her tone
and facial expressions were unnecessary and, I believe, only an
attempt to demean me. Well, it worked.*

*Interestingly enough, in almost every other setting I've had
supervisors who have treated me with respect, valuing my input.
Perhaps God is allowing things to be particularly trying here, so I
won't get too comfortable being a lawyer for this firm when I'm suppose to do something else, like helping others grow spiritually. I certainly am not helping others here.*

*After today's disappointment, I am so tempted to take off tomor-
row. I need a mental health day. But I think I'll go in—and keep
my personal days for later.*

I hope depression won't rear its ugly head again.

April 1995, when my baby was six months old, I returned
to work. Needing to pay the mortgage, I took a contractual position with an insurance company that had only employed three
to four black attorneys in its 83-year history. I was one of only
two blacks among sixteen attorneys. When I interviewed, I
sensed that I wasn't wanted there. But shucks, I needed to support my child and me. It proved to be a brutish place to work,
hostility and ill-will hung heavy in the air.

After a year of my working there, two young, childless white
males were made "permanent" during the Christmas holiday—
on the down low. When I found out about it, I fought back,
since I had been assured that new staff positions for attorneys
weren't available. Beginning with my immediate supervisor, I
talked to every person above me, including the Chief Operating
Officer. I told them that their surreptitious hiring of the two
white guys smacked of racial discrimination, and that perhaps
the EEOC would be interested in hearing about it. Soon after, I
was promoted to staff attorney and given a raise. But my three
years there were hell. I knew I had to leave. The stress was exact-
ing an enormous toll on my mental health. Like any relationship, I believe work relationships ought to be harmonious, loving, and nourishing. Mine wasn't and I knew I had to do something about it. It would take time, trust, and courage. I stepped
up my prayer, meditation and journaling. It was a life and death
situation and I wanted desperately to live.

ADDRESSING OUR GENUINE NEEDS

Can you itch but resist the impulse to scratch?

This question came to me during a meditation. I had an
insistent itch on my right cheek. I let it itch—determined to see
if I could prevail against it, to test my ability to persevere *through*

physical discomfort rather than succumb to it. Would this itch drive me insane? No. I simply needed to stay the course, to not to give in to my flesh, this flesh that knows lots of itches. An urge to shop when we need nothing in particular is an itch. The desire to get physical with someone you just met because you're enamored with him is an itch. The temptation to enter into another relationship when you should be passionately pursuing a dream is an itch. All of these itches, if not encouraged by scratching, will miraculously slip away with time.

Seldom are itches what they appear to be—authentic needs and desires. Instead they are phantom urges that beckon us to look behind them to their real source, to our heart and soul longings and needs. An intense attraction to a new man could be camouflaging a deeper need to connect with and nurture your inner man—the part of you that takes action. A powerful urge to surrender to a sexual attraction that holds no promise for the committed relationship that you say you want could be your soul yearning for an intimate connection with yourself. An insatiable appetite for sweets, alcohol or shopping might mask an authentic need to be loved and to love or a craving for creative expression. Itches are sneaky, seductive guises of the ego and flesh, not the spirit. Spirit nudges from within. The ego from without, even when it feels like an inside job. I ignored the urge to scratch my cheek. Not surprisingly, the itch gradually left me. I felt so powerful, so in control. I had wrestled with another fleshly temptation, and prevailed against it.

When you "itch," you might ask yourself, what do I *really* want? What are my genuine needs? Sure, we need safe shelter, healthy food, pure water, and clean air. But beyond these basic needs, what are our deeper emotional and spiritual longings? We need to be loved and to love. We need to grow, or else we die spiritually. We need to be seen. And heard. We need to connect with ourselves, others, and God. We need to know peace. We need to be still, to experience silence. We need to be touched, physically and emotionally. We need to create. We need to feel empowered. We need to live on purpose—if we are to experience joy, peace and authentic passion. We need to honor our needs and desires.

Behind my unrelenting itch for a man was a Pandora's box full of genuine emotional and spiritual needs, needs that no man had the capacity to fill. My deepest longing was to experience mastery over my life, to live a full, passionate life. I desperately wanted to do work that resonated in my soul, work that felt like play–but that paid well. I remain in awe of the sheer intelligence of the universe, how for every one of my deep longings a man happened along who embodied it. Early on, blinded by my neediness, I mistook him for a crutch when he was meant to be a mirror. So I'd lean, when I should have been taking in all that he reflected back to me—my good, bad, weaknesses, strengths, light and darkness— learn and grow.

My real itch was for power, authentic power, in all corners of my life. I loved law school. But prostituting myself as a hired gun for a Machiavellian insurance company, where I wasn't even welcome, was another thing altogether. Being a lawyer represented power to me, until I became one. I took pride in my accomplishment, but a sense of empowerment wasn't a natural byproduct of being an attorney. For a time, I wore my title on my sleeve, flaunting it whenever and wherever I felt a need to augment my self-image. All my years of pining for law school masked a deeper desire for a sense of being authentically powerful in the world.

I fully appreciated that it was in divine order that I attended law school. But why, I wondered, if practicing law would ultimately lack the power to make my heart sing? I refused to believe I was destined to do work that flowed against the grain of my personality and vexed my spirit. It, however, would be many years before I would stumble, seemingly, upon the truth of why I *had* to do law school.

One afternoon, I drove out to Anne Arundel County women's detention center to do a talk on taking charge of your life. A tattered paperback book sitting on a table caught my eye. It was *The Six Pillars of Self-Esteem* by Nathaniel Branden, a foremost authority on self-esteem, an author I trusted enormously on this topic. After much soul searching about why I had dedicated four years of my life to studying law only to walk away from it, Branden, with just one sentence, clarified the whole matter. In his book, Branden tells of an accomplished gentleman who'd committed many good years to trying to win his father's approval, yet he remained unhappy and unfulfilled. The reason for life, Branden wrote, is not to prove ourselves but to express ourselves. That was it! I was driven, even after my father's death, to prove wrong his dooming proclamation that I would never amount to anything. "I *would* be somebody," the wounded child in me screamed, "I will be a *lawyer!*" My becoming a lawyer wasn't about me, it was about my dad. Had it been for *me*, it would have satisfied my need to express myself through my work and sated, at least partially, my need for creative expression. My law degree represented external power. My soul yearned for authentic power. And so I began to take baby steps towards honoring my soul. That's the least I owed my restless spirit, to at least begin.

28

UNDER PARIS SKIES

*Travel does change you. We know that instinctively; it is for that,
I think, that we leave our homes and go looking for the rest of the
world. Not just to see it and know it, but to be changed by it.*

ANNE RIVERS SIDDONS

MARCH 1998 WAS GOOD TO ME. I HAPPILY RESIGNED FROM MY
job as a litigator, perfectly pleased if I never set foot into another courtroom. Never one to leap from one job to the next without at least a few days of respite and reflection in between, I flirted with the idea of jetting out of town to celebrate my new position and significant increase in salary.

SATURDAY, VALENTINE'S DAY, FEBRUARY 14, 1998
*Yesterday while chatting with Ayo in the gym, I got around to
talking about taking a vacation. We made the decision to go to Paris,
France in a couple of weeks. Paris! What's so interesting about this is
that lately, in the recent months, I'd been having involuntary fantasies about traveling to Europe. Without any attempts to do so, I'd
find myself seeing the streets of Paris. That's precisely how it unfolded back in 1989 when I went to Paris for the first time, then another time when I went to the Bahamas. I would just see myself there—
even before I'd consciously decided to visit these places. This trip
abroad will be important to my growth because it will be my first*

major trip since Adam and I ceased to be a couple. It's also important because it's consistent with how I want to spend my money and live my life. A decision I renewed recently was to travel more, to shop less. And true to my word, I've not been in a mall to shop in weeks, maybe a month. The malls are stealing our dreams. People now go to the mall like they are really going somewhere.

Tuesday, March 3, 1998

We're in Paris, France. I'm in bed. I'm tired from traveling all night.

We're back in the room. We, meaning me and Ayo, went to dinner. The attractive desk clerk, Habib, told us about a nearby restaurant. We passed on that one and found a quaint Thai restaurant around the corner. We had wine, shrimp and crabmeat. It was wonderful. Over the meal, we had a stimulating conversation.

A while later, I saw a black man enter the place. With much enthusiasm, perhaps encouraged by the wine, I excitedly shouted, "A black man!" Ayo responded, "So what?!" Little did I know this black man would be Ayo's friend who lives here in Paris, Jean-Baptiste. He came over, embraced us both. The conversation grew even more delightful. Jean-Baptiste is from Burkina Faso, West Africa. He now calls Paris home. He apparently got the voice mail that Ayo left him earlier.

When we arrived here yesterday, we took a cab from Charles de Gaulle Airport to the Regent Hotel. After the taxi driver unloaded our bags onto the street, a blond French woman—young, elegant— came to the taxi and asked in her best English, "Are you DeBora Ricks?" She explained that the hotel our agent from Mount Royal Travel had for us was under renovation and not yet finished. So this French woman booked us at another hotel, ten minutes away. Ayo told her that we were out of francs, so she said (which I believe she'd planned to do anyway) she would pay for the trip to our new hotel, Hotel Del'Esperance. It's a very lovely hotel, clean, quaint, very French. Our room is small, with twin beds though not much closet space. But it's clean, quiet and affordable, about 450 francs a day, which is about 75 U.S. dollars. It's adequate for me and Ayo. Now if our kids were here, we would have a problem. Now, when we go to Sanibel, Florida in June, we will have a condo for the five of us—mother, me and Ayo and our children, Adia and Babatunde.

The weather is quite nice here in Paris. It's warm, about 50°, sunny at times, then overcast. But no rain. Last night, we just walked until we found a nice restaurant. The bill, which I paid for with my Visa, was $211 francs, reasonable. A credit card is almost a necessity when traveling. I used it to book our hotel and last night we had no francs, so it came in handy. As I sit here on this little bed, I can't help but reflect on my life. That's the beauty of traveling. It gives you an aerial view of your life, hoping you'll see things anew.

THURSDAY, MARCH 5, 1998

It's Thursday in France. Today was sunny, mild, warm for March. Me, Ayo, and Jean-Baptiste walked to the Latin Quarter where we had lunch at the Café de Cluny, named after an old monastery that's now a museum. It's good to be back to relax in our room. Traveling in a foreign country like Paris can be taxing because of the language and cultural differences. I do believe the French are a bit like people say, not necessarily rude, but a bit arrogant—and not particularly friendly. But the people here at our hotel are very nice, very friendly. The owner is a French woman about fifty with a flare and style all her own. She's very gracious, even tries to speak English. Then there's Habib, an Arab with a unique sense of humor. I think if anything, the French seem too serious, not much laughter in their mouths. Every once in a while I would catch a French person in an uncharacteristic moment of levity. Whether they hoot it up a lot or not, the French know how to leisurely enjoy their food, friends and wine.

Again the three of us shared stimulating conversation over a fabulous dinner. Jean-Baptiste is a very interesting man. He knows Paris. He had a meeting at about 3'ish, so he left us at the café where we sat and wrote our postcards. I sent about six or seven cards back to the States.

MONDAY, MARCH 9, 1998, AIRBORNE.

Just for a moment, as I watch Paris disappear beneath us, I feel so good I could weep. I thought of my little girl Adia and how she, in her innocence and ability to live completely in the moment, is the soul sent here by God to pull me back to a life of simplicity.

This trip to Europe and the book Circle of Simplicity *has renewed my commitment to live more simply and fully. Actually, I hadn't really consciously decided to cut back on consumption for the spiritual benefits or the improved quality of my life. I'd done so to reduce my credit debt so that I could travel more. Well, now that I put it this way, I did to some extent consider how spending less money on clothes and things would allow me to improve the quality of my life via travel.*

I want to see and feel the world. I want my child to experience much of this with me. We will take long walks, eat together more, slow down and smell the roses. Voluntary simplicity—it's a choice I will make.

CITIZEN OF THE WORLD

The significance of my experience in the City of Light wasn't so much that I had journeyed there, yet again, but that I had done so on my own, unescorted by a man. It occurs to me that my true life's work has been a dogged resolve to grow up, to lay claims to me, to tap into the woman who knows who she is in all her power, glory and splendor—without a man. Adventure, curiosity, and mystery lives in me—is me—beckoning me to explore and mine them. It would be up to me to honor these passions, or die trying.

We crawl before we walk. Lean before we stand tall on our own. We compromise our grandest vision until we tap into our magnificence. It's a process. Exposure often precedes comfort. Travel enlarges us. But travel with Adam failed to satisfy my ferocious hunger to be touched, tried and tested by the experience. Always one person removed from negotiating the particulars, my travel with Adam only mildly challenged my comfort zones. I was embarrassingly like a child, always tagging along on someone else's—Adam's—adventures.

Experiences are different shared. An ambitious imagination without audacity was all I had before Adam introduced me to a bigger world. Introduction once made, the love affair blossomed. I waited with baited breath for the day I could give myself over completely to the world's exploration, unencumbered by immobilizing fears or a father figure. Now that I had a bit of disposable income on my hands and the hard earned certainty that I could handle whatever the unknown presented, I was finally ready to venture forth to fulfill a promise I'd made to myself back in 1987—to feel comfortable anywhere in the world. Why not make myself at home anywhere in the world? Am I any less a citizen of the world as any man? No, I've decided, I am not.

29

A LOVE SUPREME

Illusions die hard.

WEDNESDAY, JULY 15, 1998

Why is this happening to me? Why am I falling in love with a married man?

I want Emery, make no mistake about it. I've concluded that God is simply testing me. Emery wants me. The feeling is mutual. I like his emotional honesty, a quality that I find extremely attractive in a man. I find myself incredibly drawn to him. This man that I wish would/did have the courage to let his dead relationship with his wife go and try it with me. This is just wishful thinking; I know this intellectually. Knowing it emotionally is quite another story.

I'm not obsessing about it, I mean about Emery leaving his wife. I know he can only do this if and when he ever gets ready. No amount of talking will change that. I only wish God would stop testing me—especially in July. July seems to be a difficult time for me. It seems in July my libido is at an all-time high. I just don't get it.

MONDAY, JULY 20, 1998

Emery has got to be the sweetest man that I've met in many years. I really enjoy being with him. However, my child is acting out which makes me wonder if my love life is a mistake. Life really has its twists and turns. I was supposed to be a pretty good parent. Then my child, my almost four-year-old, showed the world what a poor parent I am by throwing a temper tantrum in the middle of Artscape, in front of a hundred of thousands of people. I'm also supposed to be beyond loving a married man—now I find myself falling head over heels for Emery. These things aren't supposed to happen to me. I'm a good person. I've got it all together. I meet men all the time. Men pursue me. I'm desired. I step over all the available men only to end up caring for a married man. Why? For one thing, Emery has more of what I want than any single man I've met recently. He's warm, funny, sweet, expressive, able to communicate, open, gentle, a good kisser, affectionate, drawn to me, wants me, needs what I have to give, and is easy going. And though he's legally married, he's not in love with his wife.

I must exercise caution here. Emery remains in a house with his wife of twenty plus years. I believe him when he says they haven't had sex in months. I'm the woman on his mind. I know this. But is this enough? No. I want Emery to be my man. I want to be able to hold his hand in public, to kiss his sweet mouth anywhere anytime, and for him to come home to me.

A TENDER, LOVING AND KIND MAN

Tenderness, a quality my heart ached to find in a man, was perhaps Emery's most compelling strength. Somehow he understood what few brothers do—that tenderness is not a weakness that compromises one's manhood, but rather a fundamental quality that makes him more fully a man. His perfect smile was reflected in his eyes and lit up my heart. Intelligence, emotional honesty and the ability to communicate his deepest feelings struck me as rare enough qualities in a man for me to rethink my position on loving a married man. He gave me no roses, but he still was a hopeless romantic. Our time spent together didn't demand that we go anywhere or do anything to resonate with meaning. We were our own happiness, our own joy. Embellishments of any kind were superfluous. Our intimacy transcended our bodies, locking us together as souls. Everything we shared felt intimate, sacred, soulful—from our quietly passionate discussions on history, politics, music and life—to the hand in hand strolls through exotic gardens or black art exhibits.

All that Emery and I shared were intensely charged moments of sheer sensual pleasure that lingered with me for days. Incredibly, I'd finally met a man who, like me, genuinely delighted in life's simple beauty, magic and mystery. And he was in love with me. I appreciated the seriousness of what I was doing. I was in it for the long haul. Or so I felt.

SATURDAY, JULY 25, 1998

Emery and I are an item. I've decided to go ahead and love this man, this married man. I have no regrets, feel no shame, and have few reservations. We're meant to be, if not forever then certainly for the present and foreseeable future.

The man cares about me. Yes, he's legally married to Linda (he said her name last night) but his heart and body are mine. I've been with my share of men and Emery perhaps is one of the few, if not the only one, who I really believe when he tells me he cares, that he's my man, that he's faithful to me, that I'm special to him. In other words, I trust this man.

I didn't trust Adam—but Emery I trust. I'm not willing to give that up. I'm simply unwilling to walk away from a man who actually tells me how he feels. Emery is the man I've been dreaming about all these years. Emery is it. He's lots of fun to be with. I love to hear him laugh. We laugh a lot together, too. He has a brain that can form opinions. I love that. He's smart. He's reliable. He's passionate. He's got sweet kisses. He's generous. I simply love his perfect smile. He's honest. Kind. He's all man. He's gentle. We have so much in common that it's as if we're the same person. Just like me, he's glad—very glad—that we met.

Despite Emery's marital status, I sincerely believe we're meant for each other. Oh, I know I said I would no longer deal with or get involved with a married man. This is different. On the surface, what we're doing seems, or maybe is, wrong. Emery is legally married. I'm not interfering with anything though. One reason I steered clear of married men was because I believe it's wrong to disrupt a married man's life with his wife and children. But Emery sleeps in one room and Linda sleeps in the basement. They share only a house and grown offspring. There's no love between them. Maybe they get along, but Emery is the kind of man who needs to be loved passionately, deeply.

I'm not rationalizing either. I know this is based not only on what Emery has shared with me, but also what I can sense, feel and see. I'm not just a conquest to Emery. For so many years, he's gone unloved, uncared for. He, like all of us, needs to be held, kissed, appreciated, touched, admired, loved. This man isn't getting any of that with his wife. Some married men only want a piece on the side—another reason I avoid them. Well, I'm so much more than that to Emery.

WEDNESDAY, AUGUST 5, 1998

Good morning, God!

I should be writing to God, instead I want to write about the new love of my life. Well, therein lies a part of the problem. I'm doing the very thing James Redfield cautioned against in his book, The Celestine Prophecy. *I'm turning further away from the true Source of my power and blessings, and turning too much toward Emery. I've really got to be careful about this.*

THURSDAY, AUGUST 6, 1998

You reach an impasse in a relationship, whether personal or professional, when one or both sides is demanding something more—but neither party is willing to give any more. Emery and I are at an impasse. Actually, we're on the way out. At least at the time of our last meeting, that's exactly where we were.

He decided we wouldn't work because, to say it more directly than he did, he wants to f— me and I won't let him. He wants to screw my brains out, get up, put his pants, on and go home to the wife he keeps in the basement. I say no. That's just a bridge I'm not ready to cross. I love him. I love him more than I can remember loving any man. But I love me too. And what about some self-respect here? He wants more without giving more. I can't do it. At least not now. Never say never, but right now, in this moment, I say no. We're through. Done.

30

FAST FORWARD

Real love is a permanent self-enlarging experience.
                    M. SCOTT PECK, *The Road Less Traveled*

FRIDAY, AUGUST 7, 1998

This is Day One of my 21-day fast. It's going well. I meditated and prayed this morning. It makes a difference. As the sister at the fasters' meeting said last night, prayer doesn't necessarily change the situation, it changes you. I know.

I've had a beautiful day with Adia. It was the Morning Prayer. I also think my praying has been the reason I've not been hungry though it's 7:35 p.m. I've been drinking distilled water all day. I ate two organic pears and a very good salad that I bought from the Village Market.

I talked to Emery last night from about 10ish to 1 a.m. We love each other. We're so connected. It feels incredibly satisfying, which causes me to sometimes wonder if our affinity for each other isn't problematic. Are we seeking something from each other that we ought to either look to the Creator for or within ourselves? Admittedly, our staying on the phone all through the night when we should be getting some sleep is a problem. But with so few hours to "live" after the workday is done, what do people like us do? I guess it helps if you live together. I guess.

Emery and I had a steamy, interesting conversation over the phone today. He got to see my feisty side. He says I'm aggressive. He was especially low key, maybe even down. He called it "flat." Anyway, we were on opposite ends of the emotional continuum. I could feel him. I could feel me wanting him to be different, wanting him to be more motivated to do the things that would help him change some of the stuff in his life. He's been working for the same people for two decades, a long, long time. As he frequently reminds me, he takes the path of least resistance. So this morning Emery comments that he's thinking about pursuing another master's degree.

Oh, I know what that's about. That's the easy way out. A lot of people return to school, especially those who seek multiple advanced degrees, when they get the urge to make a life change—when they can't seem to muster the courage to do what they really need to do to move their life forward. A structured environment like a university gives us the sense that we're doing something constructive, meaningful and upwardly mobile, while providing the external pressures to get it done. Self-motivation can be hard to generate when we are afraid. Jumping out there on our own demands that we set our own parameters; that's difficult to do when you have difficulty self-validating. We must structure our lives without the external forces that school provides. That's a challenge many people aren't up to taking on.

These twenty-one days will test us, me and Emery. We discussed that this morning, which is another reason Emery moves me. In fact, it's probably the major reason I want to be with this man. He expresses himself. He's honest with me. We share an intimacy that I've never been able to cultivate with any other man. I cannot think of one man in my past that so consistently and candidly shared his feelings and thoughts. Emery does this, and boy is it the sweetest, sweetest thing.

Anyway, we could already feel the pull. I was up, way up. Clear. Zooming. Emery was lethargic. We didn't fight. I don't have to fight with a man who tells himself the truth—and is able to let me hear him do it. I'm sure—we're sure—this fast will cause some tension between us as I get clearer, stronger and feel more empowered. Emery's shortcomings, especially those that are also my demons, will become glaringly apparent during this time.

I must resist the urge to try and change him, but instead keep the focus on myself. We both said patience would be required. I must say I'm so glad this is something I will be experiencing with the man I love. Sure, I wish he would join me in the fast. I invited him today. He didn't say yes or no. I got the feeling he thought it wasn't for him. This is how he was about seeing Iyanla Vanzant, reticent. Then that night as Ayo and I walked toward the Walter's Art Gallery, I looked up to see a familiar car turn the corner coming toward us. It was Emery. I thought excitedly, "He came!" as I smiled to myself. I was glad to discover he wasn't the kind of man who refuses to put himself in the presence of truth.

I had a realization this morning, a thought that had occurred to me several times before, but this time I really got it. The reason Emery is a married man, but is no longer emotionally involved with his wife (I started to write "connected" in the place of "involved," but he is connected) is because neither of us is ready for a fully committed relationship. I want a relationship without the responsibility of having to take care of a man. That's a lot of work, and perhaps I'm still afraid of losing myself in a man. That's why we've not had intercourse, because once I've let a man enter me, I tend to lose myself in him. I lose my ability to be objective. I become clingy, possessive, demanding. I don't like the woman I become. I lose my perspective, which I cannot afford to do.

With Emery, I get most of what I want and need in a man minus the domestic work. I don't mind that Emery goes home every night. In fact, if I were to get real honest, I would admit that I want him to go home every night. It's a chore trying to coexist with another person in the morning, trying to get me to work and Adia to Mother's. I'm simply not ready to share my home fully with a man. Now with a new and "improved" (as in bigger) house I might feel different. Once I'm truly ready to allow a man to completely share my life, then the universe will send me a man who is free to love me, without the encumbrances. This man probably will not be Emery. The truth is, Emery will probably stay in his situation for a lifetime.

31

WILLING BUT NOT READY

Genuine intimacy cannot thrive where addiction is present.
LORNA HOCHSTEIN, PH.D.

IN DRUID HILL PARK ~

Now that I understand why I chose Emery to be the man in my life, I graciously accept our limitations. He's not wrong. Nor am I. We're just where we are. Neither of us can yet handle a full-time, fully committed relationship—and that's really okay. I can't wait to share this revelatory thought with Emery. Now perhaps we can just relax and enjoy each other.

Emery professed his love for me this morning. My phone rang about 2 a.m. It was my lover, Emery. My caller ID indicated he'd called earlier, before I arrived home from my friend Mark's party. I love the ring of that phone, when I know it's the man I love.

As usual, we talked quite a while. Like no other time that I can remember, Emery said he loved me, that he couldn't imagine me not being a part of his life. I truly love the way this man loves. He tells me he's got to do better expressing himself with words. I haven't noticed a problem. He's so much more expressive than any man I've ever related to that I can't complain. We talk. We actually share thoughts, feelings, hopes, fears.

When Emery talks, I listen. His words are like jewels. My soul is so very satisfied with this man. I don't seek to change him. I just want to love him, to be here for him. I told him many things last night as I lay in bed, in the dark. I asked him if he felt me being protective, and if that was a problem. He said "no." At forty-some-thing, he's never been protected. He was always the one people expected to be the protector. Well, I feel very protective of this man. I don't baby him too much. But I'm clear, as I told him, that all of us need the same thing—to be accepted, loved, and sometimes pro-tected. Knowing Emery lost both his parents as a small child—I can't help but want to hold him, run my fingers through his hair, and make everything better. He's my baby. I can feel his need to be loved in every possible way a man could be loved. I have that need to do it. He likes it, he said, when I rub his head. I asked him what it is he's telling me when he kisses me. We both agree that words fail to say what the heart deeply feels.

I love the man. I love him the way I'd only dreamed of loving a man. He's sweet. He trusts me. That means the world to me. His trust lets me know he knows my love for him is real. I told him I might be predictable because I want him to be able to count on me. That's important to me because I've been let down so much. Not because these men had a change of heart, but because most never intended to be the man he professed to be. He may have had an agenda. He wanted "some," so the man would say and do almost anything toward that end. Then there have been the times when I was with a man only for what he could do for me. My heart wasn't in it. I couldn't care less about his needing me. I had my needs to fulfill. That's all that mattered to me. I had only hoped that would be enough for him.

But it's different with Emery. I told Emery about my revelation last night, that I don't want, or I'm apparently not ready for, any relationship that would require all of me, that he's what I need. That the limitations we have are okay because obviously I'm not ready for a completely available man, else I would have attracted one. Emotionally, I am not there. Emery said he was surprised at my words. We both hoped that when each of us is ready to participate fully in a relationship, we would be the beneficiaries of that new emotional readiness. I certainly could see being with Emery for many years to come because the sharing and caring is the best yet. We're always respectful of each other. Even when we "fight," it never gets ugly. I care too much to do that. Besides, after the fight, I still want to be able to look into my guy's eyes. I mustn't be a destructive force in his life.

SUNDAY, AUGUST 16, 1998

We worked it out. My love and I are no longer at odds with each other. This love is what I love between us. There's a gentleness that's between us that just feels so nurturing, so nourishing. Emery, with his superb ability to express his emotions, is so loving, so sweet. I'm glad we weather our various storms without tearing each other up and down in the process.

Speaking of process. Emery, when we fight, pulls away to process his pain. After several attempts on my part to bridge the emotional gap, and no signs of his willingness to talk, I get frustrated and hurt. Instead of seeing Emery as being in his process mode, I feel he's gone too far. His silence then becomes punitive. That's his challenge.—to not do that. Yesterday, I think he could feel me move on emotionally without him. I figured, if he wants to pout and punish, well then, so be it. Life goes on. I went upstairs and put music on, Baaba Maal's Nomad Soul. My spirit started dancing, then my feet followed. This young African brother's beautiful music entered my soul, massaged it, then transported it to a higher spiritual plane. I left Emery right where he was, sulking downstairs.

As I lay here, journaling, with barely any clothes on, my thoughts fell on my Emery, my sweet, sweet man. I looked at my bare, lean, strong thighs and thought of Emery's tender touch, his sweet lips caressing my skin. Here is a man who treats me just the way I've longed to be treated. He respects me as a woman. He also babies me. With Emery, I'm able to experience so many emotions. I love it. He frustrates me sometimes, but when we aren't being challenged by one of life's many and expected challenges, we're flowing together like a body of water—like the ebb and flow of the ocean we groove.

Emery takes care of me. The other night we'd fallen asleep on the sofa, his head in my lap, when suddenly Adia screams, "Mommy, I need you!" Startled, I leapt up. In an instant, Emery gently stopped me, quietly whispered for me to ease up. I listen to Emery because I respect and love this man. He loves and respects me. Before Emery left, as usual, he made sure all the downstairs windows were closed and locked.

Men. They compartmentalize their lives so much that they divorce themselves from themselves. And then of course, they have no idea who the hell they are. Adam is the master of compartmentalization. Emery, it just hit me, does it too. He lives on one street and loves on another. But then, what does that say about me for loving Emery? Didn't I endure this with Adam? Though I tell myself this is different because I don't really want all of any man, is it really different? Is it? Or is this a mere rationalization? I really don't know.

What I do know is that I don't care for the burden of having a man 24/7. I do not wish to take care of a man's every single need—cooking for him, cleaning behind him, washing all his clothes. Nor do I wish to have to take care of a man's need for a lot of assurance, any incessant need for validation, give too much time, or hold his hand too much. The other good stuff—making love, war and emotional sharing—are joys, especially with Emery. But some men get really clingy. With Emery, that's really a sign that he's not living enough, moving ahead.

Emery is brilliant. He knows a lot about a lot. But he's suffering from a serious case of inertia. I hope he wasn't exercising and reading—until he met me. No, I doubt it. I do think however he loves loving so much right now that he's being consumed by it. I understand. I was too. Until I began my fast. Coupled with the very spiritually nourishing Thursday night meetings, this has been a real *re-charger for me. I only wish Emery had whatever it takes to do it with me. I don't quite understand some people. He turns down my invitation to work out with me at the gym. Time together, I figured, and a chance to get fit. Then there is the 21-day fast he declined to participate in. He's just too damn resistant.*

Men. Too many of them have no spiritual path to speak of. That's what I need: a spiritual, emotional, intelligent, evolving, healthy, happy, loving, kind, generous, sexy, funny man. I thought Emery was it, or at least interested in getting back on a path. Maybe he is. I need to just relax and leave the man alone, just love him. If it happens, we have a better chance at being together, staying together. If it doesn't, it will be difficult. I think he's afraid to go into my social circles. Oh, I don't know! And there's no point in trying to figure him out. In time, I'll know all I need to know.

32

GONE TOO SOON

I've never seen a case of love addiction where the love addict was relatively happy with his or her life.

IRENE MATIATOS, PH.D.

SUNDAY, SEPTEMBER 20, 1998

Emery and I are no more. Our argument on last Sunday ushered in the end of us. I shouted something like, "You must be looking for a superwoman!" To which he angrily replied, "No, just a woman who is super in ways you aren't!"

So what made me get involved with him? Was it my belief that love can heal all things? Yes. And no. I took Emery's ability to self-express, to share his emotions honestly as a sign that he was at least on the path toward wholeness. So when he began to try and dictate what we would talk about, I knew it was time to cut him loose. All we had was communication!

In a relationship with a man, soul satisfying communication means more to me than his having money. That's why it didn't matter to me that Emery didn't have any money. It was what he gave of himself that made me want him, over and over again, until what I got was only his ugly side.

I'm not yet sure why Emery came into my life, but one thing he leaves with me is hope. I now know it is possible for a man to be gentle, sweet and loving—even though Emery couldn't sustain it.

What Emery shared with me was so special. That's exactly what I'm going to hold out for, only this time I will only be available to a single, emotionally available man who can sustain it.

Two to three months into the typical romantic interlude, the sugar goes. It is at this time that the other foot accompanies the proverbial best foot, introducing us to the other side of our beloved, a side we'd naively expected never to surface. It can look a lot like the old bait and switch at play, but it's not. It's simply the anatomy of romantic love. It flows then ebbs, waxes then wanes, then flows anew when we nurture and work at it. Once the new relationship smell wears off, we come face to face with the real man we fell in love with and the pivotal question: do we jump ship now or do we stay and work toward authentic love? That is, love based not on who we appear to be, but who we truly are.

Hooked on the sweetness, many women endure untold indignities and abuse waiting for, they insist, the return of the good guy they fell in love with. For the severely wounded, the other foot is frequently a concrete wall erected to keep their beloved from getting any closer, from seeing their faults and failures, real or imagined.

Emery started diminishing me. In our most intimate moments, he'd do or say hurtful things, things that turned me away from him. He began shutting down, limiting and circumscribing our once fulfilling conversations. Everything meaningful went. A closet passive-aggressive, he'd deny feelings of hurt and anger only to later launch a vicious sneak attack on my self-esteem—attacks he'd flat out deny—while accusing me of having out of control insecurities or a hypersensitive mind. He'd do what men do when they really want to disarm a woman, disparage my looks by comparing me with other women—always to my detriment. The very qualities that enamored me to this sensuous man—attentiveness, sensitivity to my feelings, openness and emotional fluidity—seemed to rapidly evaporate.

STAND BY YOUR LOVING MAN

There are no perfect relationships. No unions without conflict and challenges. Difficulties faced, tackled and worked through create a pathway to healing and growth for both individual and couple. Emotional abuse, however, isn't an imperfection any couple can afford to tolerate. "You know how I am. I told you I say stupid things!" Emery would plea. "A good woman stands by her man, no matter what," his argument went. Had Emery fully owned his abusive behaviors, recognized them as unacceptable, and endeavored to change them, I might have foolishly invested more of myself in this wrong-from-the-start-relationship.

With an available man—as in single, stable in mind, and committed to spiritual evolution—it can make sense for two people to work through their demons. Some of them. It's a case-by-case decision a woman must make. Fact is, to paraphrase author James Baldwin, a man can't fix what he won't face. If he denies or repeatedly excuses his abusive treatment of you, don't waste your precious time with him. A man will never change behaviors he doesn't view as a problem.

I was wrong to get involved with a married man. It was wrong for all concerned—my child, Emery, his wife, his offspring and me. Addicts are selfish people. What they want is the driving force behind most, if not all, decisions they make. The most loving thing an addict can do for herself and her loved ones is to diligently channel her life force into self-recovery.

The tantrum my preschooler threw at the summer arts festival was her way of demanding that I give her the love and attention that I was lavishing on Emery. I intuitively knew it then, but I wanted what I wanted. Feeling powerless to escape the horror of my job situation, I opted for a short cut to ecstasy—a new man. I hated wasting my time and energies day in and day out in a position ill-suited to my talents and passions. I felt trapped and feared making a change. Clever old ego seduced me into thinking, once again, that if I couldn't be whole at least I could be loved.

Love, true love, flows from wholeness. Reaching for a relationship to fill the empty places inside us isn't love but addiction and abuse, a clever attempt to avoid the labor pains every soul must endure if it is to give birth to its authenticity. If love is "the will to extend oneself for hers or another's spiritual growth," to paraphrase author M. Scott Peck's definition of true love, then love demands infinitely more than many of us are willing to give.

Immediate gratification is the enemy of true love. I wanted to feel good, so I entered into an unholy relationship. Though I sincerely adored Emery, it was my unconscious desire to compensate for the lack of sweetness in my work—and the fear that what my soul deeply desired was impossible for me—that drove me into the arms of this married man. When we love ourselves enough to commit to pursuing our deepest passions and purpose, our self-esteem soars. Then we are not only better able to resist temptation, but we'll respect our time, our energy, and ourselves too much to squander them on dishonoring liaisons and dead-end jobs. I was in a job I despised, but instead of expending my energies on finding and living my purpose, I settled for a counterfeit love. Emery, instead of pouring his efforts into making his marriage work or mustering the courage to release it, sought to sweeten the pot ever so often with a new honey. These were cowardly choices.

MAKING HARD CHOICES MOVE US FORWARD

There is no escaping it. If we are to leave addiction behind, grow in peace, and experience joy, we've got to make hard choices that push us beyond the easy and comfortable. It can be a narrow, difficult road but it leads us to our wholeness and purpose.

There I was, finally earning a living wage only to have to face the bitter truth that I deeply hated what I did and where I was. Problem was, I never did fit in. Bureaucracy and I have never made for a happy marriage. Every workday of suffering, I'd again ask myself "why am I choosing to bring my body to this hideous place?"

One day at work, during a conversation with a coworker and friend, Henry, I got an answer to my prayer for direction and strength. Spirit whispered, "*If you are unhappy here, don't you understand that I have a better place for you? If you will do the work that you were born to do, that work will sustain you.*" It's not God's will that we suffer a job. We are meant to experience fulfillment in all facets of our life. My belief that no one would match—or maybe exceed—my salary for me to do what I love was not based in reality but rooted in fear. I began working with the Truth—God is my Source. God is my Source. God is my Source. All good flows from God, my Source. I needed only to trust.

33

I Can't Stand the Pain

In order to pursue an addiction, individuals must progressively abandon themselves.

Anne Wilson Schaef

Friday, September 25, 1998

I wanted to believe that getting over and beyond Emery would be easy. At least I think I can do it, without going back on my promise not to be with anyone who isn't kind to me. I've kept my promise so far. But I'm paying a price for leaving.

I'm shopping like crazy. That zero balance I had on my Visa is now probably over $1,000. And I haven't been taking very good care of my body. I haven't worked out in a couple of weeks. My body also needs hydration. Why I haven't bought any water is beyond me—or is it? I'm not even eating regularly. I've managed to avoid eating meats again, but I've put plenty of sugar into my body.

I know what's wrong. The realization struck me today. I'm trying to medicate my hurt with things. Problem with that is I keep craving more and more stuff. Admittedly, some of the stuff I had planned to get with my tax refund are some I even need. Well, I'm still shopping because I miss my Emery terribly.

I put Aaron Neville's CD on because he helps me feel the pain. I want to feel it, all of it. I think I'm ready to pull-up on the spending, to take care of me again. It's going to take effort. I should be *proud of myself nonetheless. I've not resorted to calling Emery, at least not since Monday. I also deserve a pat on the back because I'm smart enough to move on, rather than accept the emotional abuse that he was beginning to dole out. He's also hurting. My friend Claudia saw him yesterday. She said he looked so sad. He probably thought I would stay around, despite his cruel treatment of me— like the old me would have done a few years ago.*

We all want companionship. I'm no different. I can't, however, tolerate hostility and cruelty. I've had more than my share of that. I'm still looking for the man with a slow hand, a tender heart, and some kind words for me. I want to be a man's baby, friend, lover, sister, partner and more. (Not necessarily in that order though.)

Emery frequently asked me, "Why do you stay with me?" It was simple: no longer needing a man's financial assistance and no longer convinced that the measure of my worth was determined by how much a man gave me, I was in it for love. The more tender the better. I also need honest communication. Gradually Emery withdrew all of that. That's when the arguments started. He would say things that were supposedly harmless—but were laced with malice. With time, his words began to poison our relationship, destroying my love for him.

GATHERING MY THOUGHTS

Healing is a protracted process of purging that takes hyper-vigilance and patience. It's about gradually becoming whole—unto oneself. It's about reclaiming every part of yourself—mind, body and spirit—piece by piece, until you are the master of your life. Emery showed me how vulnerable I was, how unhealed my mind remained. I foolishly believed it was okay to get involved with this man, since his marriage had hit a brick wall years before he laid eyes on me. Since his emancipated child was out of the house away at college. Since he was painfully unhappy. Since there burned an intense fire between us.

Rationalization is the weapon of the enemy—addiction. Whenever I find myself rationalizing my behavior, I know

I've entered the danger zone and was dangerously close to slipping into an addictive, self-destructive pattern. Thank God I've journaled faithfully, else it might have taken me significantly longer to wade through the s—- my ego had me knee deep in. Once again, my beloved was but a mirror reflection of me, my troubled spots, my soul's longing to grow. Emery was likely the sweetest, gentlest man that I'd known. Our soul demands sweetness and tenderness and beauty. Emery brought a sweetness to my life and unwittingly showed me how necessary it was for me to cultivate more sweetness within and around me.

But this brilliantly talented man was stuck. He was stuck in a marriage, job and lifestyle that no longer served his highest good. He'd been languishing in a dead-end job for more than two decades. Like a helpless little boy, he cowered and whined as his superiors shuffled and played him like a cheap deck of cards. I'd grown smart enough to know one thing for sure—Emery came to teach me something about me. Three months before we met, I'd started working a job where none of what I desired to give to the world they wanted. I immediately sensed that Emery was who I would become—twenty years later—if I let fear keep me from pursuing my dreams. I knew this was the real reason Emery came, so he could be a glimpse into the future that awaited me if I didn't think enough of myself to follow my heart. The choice was mine: I could let a $60,000 salary tempt me to settle, or I could step out on faith and walk toward my deepest heart's desires.

Emery's tongue-in-cheek mantra, "I take the path of least resistance," was his attempt to justify his survivalist choices. And, as I assured him, that is indeed the path paved with the fewest rewards. He was terrified, he confessed, of change. I understood. Ghosts from his lonely childhood still haunted him, duping him into treating phantoms as if they were real. I, too, was scared of the unknown. But not risking, settling for what I could see, frightened me significantly more.

Even the slightest open psychic wounds distort our sight and threaten to derail our sincerest intentions. Knowing wholeness and experiencing that wholeness at your very core is the best protection against foolish, sabotaging choices. I had to be smarter—married men came off my list of potential partners.

I came to appreciate the critical connection between addiction, fear and feelings of powerlessness. We're vulnerable to acting out addictively when we let fear keep us from taking risks on behalf of our dreams. I hated my job. I felt trapped and powerless. My soul craved peace and purpose. Taking charge of my career, that is, leaving a spirit-annihilating job, would have empowered me. But that road was intimidating, so I fearfully chose the path of least resistance—I entered into yet another ill-fated relationship. I wasn't off the hook though. Emery's sad life forced the issue. I chose again. This time, I chose to feel the fear and do what I feared anyway.

Almost a year to my date of hire, March 1999, I would resign from my state job. I lost two thirds of my salary but what I gained in courage, resolve and self-respect made up for it. I'd honored the wishes of my higher self, putting myself one step closer to living a life that I could love.

34

IT'S A THIN LINE

*Anger is rooted in judgment. We hold others to some standard
that we have somehow fantasized, chosen, and applied to them.
They may not even know about these standards, but that does
not matter to us.*

BRIAN WEISS, M.D., *Messages from the Masters*

SUNDAY, SEPTEMBER 27, 1998

*As I review my journal entries, I'm struck by the frequency with
which I got in and out of relationships. I feel ashamed. I'm not sure
if I want to put this out there in the universe for everyone to see. But
what's most disturbing, ten years later, is that it seems I'm still getting into these short-term relationships that don't work. I really can't
afford to do this. I'm a mother. I don't want my little girl to relate
to men this way. I do take some time between men, unlike ten years
ago, but I really need to just chill on getting involved altogether for
some time.*

I repeat, every relationship reveals us. Our beloved is but a
reflection of us. Yes, I was no longer afraid of being alone. But
like any heterosexual woman, my desire for a companionable
man persisted. In and out of relationships I went. But still, more
often than not, I found myself settling for what I *didn't* want,
compromising on my stated values. I concluded that it was time

I examined and reexamined my beliefs about men, specifically my attitudes about black men. It's shockingly revealing, but here are the toxic beliefs that I've held about brothers.

- Men aren't interested in love, just sex.
- Men are one dimensional, shallow creatures.
- Men don't know how to communicate.
- Men can't cope.
- Men fear commitment.
- Men always cheat.
- Men can't be trusted.
- Men are angry and hostile.
- Men are selfish and weak.
- Men are rough and mean.
- Men are irresponsible.
- Men are terrified of feelings, theirs and others'.
- Men can't be relied upon. When things get tough, men get going.
- Men are intimidated by smart, educated, empowered women.
- Men move from woman to woman so as to avoid intimacy with themselves and others.
- Men don't read.
- Men are superficial.
- Men aren't committed to any spiritual path.

YOUNG MEN, WHITE MEN

In my youth, I worshipped men. To my childlike mind, men were deity, worthy of veneration and praise. Strong. Compelling. Infallible. Full of power and possibility. I zigzagged toward womanhood, full of hope and unreasonable expectations. I loved hard, with all of my everything. I got hurt a lot. Then the pendulum swung the other way, heaving the entire male world from grace into an abyss. Love turned into hate. Years of hurt, disappointment, betrayal, loss, abuse, misuse and resentment calcified into seething contempt and bitterness for an entire segment of the population.

Men, especially black men, became the enemy. I blamed them for everything that went or could go wrong in love. They became the repository into which I dumped all of my despair over love that had turned sour. It was men's fault that love didn't survive beyond the gaga-love-is-blind stage. I denied all responsibility—for my neediness and the unwanted experiences that flowed from it. I—she who insists there is no such thing as victimhood—felt like the proverbial victim.

My noxious notions about men, coupled with my self-esteem issues, were the driving force behind my failed relationships. As long as I believed the worst about men, no matter how good I felt about me, I was doomed to disappointment and loss in love.

Living without intimacy and love, however, did not strike me as a very appealing option, so I considered my alternatives. I entertained an increasingly popular choice for women—loving another woman. I actually went through a period when I deliberately worked on seeing women as possible lovers and partners. If it were in me to do, I suppose my mental foray into lesbianism would have resulted in a real life adventure. But it was not in me. There's a certain something about testosterone that I find supremely irresistible. Truth is, I'm hopelessly hooked on that seductively sweet dance that naturally occurs between the yin and the yang, a man and a woman.

I examined two other possibilities, younger men and white men. I concluded that a younger man comes with less oppressive baggage, isn't as competitive with or threatened by an empowered woman, and is more comfortable with emotional vulnerability—his and other's. The opportunity to explore interracial dating had presented itself years earlier, before I was at ease with making this bold choice. Fact is a man is a man is a man. Whether black, white, young or mature every man—as does every human being—has issues and baggage.

It's decidedly a woman's prerogative to date and love whomever she so desires. My loyalty would be to me. I see no reason to limit my options in any way. Power is all about having options, many and varied.

I understood, intellectually at least, that my exasperation with men reflected the relationship that I was in with myself. It hurt nonetheless that men so often let me down, broke my heart, or came up short emotionally, intellectually or spiritually. It took the love of a few true friends to help me appreciate that the ugliness that I saw in men was alive in my head. Consequently, I couldn't help but draw what I *didn't* want to me, over and over again.

While my heart was burdened by hate, I had the good fortune to work with several extraordinary brothers who were quietly committed to building community, loving relationships, and personal growth. I had to assume that if there was even one honorable, loving black man out there, then there had to be more. Appreciating the connection between what materialized in my life and my core beliefs, I endeavored to assume more responsibility, once again, for what I was creating. If other women were attracting decent, loving, committed black men then I had better look within me, to what I believed about my possibilities and myself in love.

I've had to admit that so many of my bad relationship choices stemmed from my tendency to settle. I didn't believe it was possible to have all that I wanted in a man. Consequently, I always seemed to couple with men who had at least one fatal flaw. He'd be handsome, attentive, loving but unemployed and unfocused. Or he'd be smart, ambitious and financially secure but emotionally absent. Where, I wondered, are the honest, kind, smart, forward thinking, good looking, commitment-ready, emotionally available, spiritual men? I honestly didn't know, but regardless, I knew one thing for certain—I had to stop settling.

I had to stop settling for what I *don't* want. I had to stop entering hollow, shallow alliances when what I really yearned for was an abiding spiritual partnership. I needed to stop confusing sexual intensity with love and intimacy. I had to reject emotionally challenged lads and wait for the emotionally available man, for as long as it took. I've had to quit sleep walking into wrong-from-the-start liaisons, foolishly expecting it to one day miraculously meet my needs. I am learning to not just read the writing on the wall, but to use it as the basis for deciding whether a man is a good fit or not. And if he's not, no matter how sexy, fine or attentive he is, I am learning to just say, "no." If it doesn't fit, I will not force it. I have learned, at last, how to be "alone" and love it.

Cluttering up our world with what we *don't* want keeps those people and things we *do* want from making their way to us. When a woman genuinely believes she deserves nothing but the best, she starts to really dance to the beat of her own drums, learns to just say "no" to men who are clearly wrong for her, and thus creates space in her consciousness and life for her ultimate good.

35

SLIPPED INTO DARKNESS

Fear is a noose that binds until it strangles.

JEAN TOOMER

WEDNESDAY, NOVEMBER 25, 1998

I'm lower than I've been in a long time. In fact, I can't remember the last time I felt so low. It's the kind of low that interferes even with my ability to think and feel. I feel numb, dull, out of touch. I've got to call it depression because that's what it feels like. Even after getting an invitation from my good friend Sheila to go to Hawaii with her, I'm still down. This is an all-time low for me.

FRIDAY, NOVEMBER 27, 1998

I think I'm beginning to feel better, less depressed.

SUNDAY, NOVEMBER 29, 1998

I'm in my active addiction. It's really got me going. I just need to write to try and shake whatever is making me think shopping will make me feel better, make me BE better. Something's definitely going on with me. I'm not completely sure what. Maybe I'm unhappy. No, not maybe, I AM unhappy. I am unhappy with me. It's DeBora I don't like so much right now. I feel a lot of shame at work. And it's not helping that I am no longer exercising. I will today. Instead of saying I will start today, I will simply take one day at a

time, and do at least one physical activity a day. I don't like not tak-
ing care of me. It only adds to my self-loathing. Self-loathing. Why?
Why must so many people, especially women, loathe themselves? For
me, I think I feel a lot of shame about not living up to who I know
I am. What am I waiting for, permission? No one's going to give me
that, no one but me.

I've got to, no—I WILL *behave my way out of this funk I'm in.*
It's a question of self-worth. That wonderful movie based on Amy
Tan's book, The Joy Luck Club, *reminded me of this last night. I*
was in the stores too long. Got home, heated up the Thanksgiving
leftovers, put pictures in an empty album, and watched this very
interesting and enlightening movie about the hopes, struggles, pains
and joys of a group of Asian women. The one all-important thing
that I got from the movie was that a woman, without the assistance
of a man—or for that matter, society—must know her own worth.
A man cannot give a woman worth, but a woman can give her
worth away. A woman can forget who and what she is, especially
when she couples with a man. She must be particularly vigilant at
such times. And she must never apologize for who she is. Never.

Earlier, before I left home, I had a breakthrough. I took a warm
bath with two lighted candles. As I dried my body, I thought about
what one of the older women in The Joy Luck Club *told her*
daughter. Her daughter had done what millions of women do—
she'd forsaken herself in her marriage. For six years, she focused her
energies on trying to make her successful publisher husband happy.
She tried to anticipate his every need and desire. What she'd forgot-
ten, however, was that what made him happy was to share his life
with another whole person. He pleaded with her to tell him what
she wanted. He said he missed hearing her voice, that is, her uncen-
sored opinions. He missed hearing the woman she was whether or
not that pleased him. That scene made me think of Adam. And
interestingly, just moments ago, I read a little more of Necessary
Losses *by Judith Viorst. She wrote about people who present a false*
self to the world, chameleons. Adam was both.

I remember telling him to get in touch with himself. Like the
woman in the movie, Adam expended most of his energies trying to

anticipate my every want and need—so he could make me happy—
when all I wanted, and I constantly told him so, was for him to be
himself. A person who "builds his entire existence around a false self
suffers from the spiritual burden of not appearing as the person he
is, or not being the person he appears to be," writes Viorst. Boy, is
that a perfect description of Adam, which is why I could no longer
be with him. One inevitably begins to feel lonely with such people.

Okay, back to the breakthrough. As I toweled my body, I
remembered that Asian mother telling her confused daughter that
she must know her own worth. I began to say those words out loud
to myself, "You must know your own worth, you must know your
own worth, you must know your own worth." Then the tears came.
I can feel something welling up in my chest even now as I write. I
am remembering who and whose I am. I am worth something—
and it's quite a lot. I've got to stop looking to others to tell me what
I'm worth—no one else knows, except my Creator. Today I will be
like the chrysanthemum that blooms after long periods of darkness—I will blossom and flower. And if someone should find me
pleasing to look at, to be with, to know—I say Amen. If they don't,
so be it.

36

THE POWER OF CHOICE

Don't confuse tough choices with no choices at all.

CHERYL RICHARDSON

TUESDAY, DECEMBER 1, 1998

I am on my way out. I'm putting irons in the fire. I'm telling people I'm leaving. After a lot of thought yesterday, I concluded that if I'm going to leave this decent paying job, for less money no doubt, then at least I ought to have more freedom, more flexibility, more time to write. Therefore, I'm looking for a position, whatever, where I can work just three days a week. The other two days, I'll write and go to the gym. I'm going to live the life I envision for myself—not this boring, institutional life—or die trying.

THURSDAY, DECEMBER 3, 1998

We have a choice—as to how we live our life. Then why do so many of us live as if we don't? Knowing or realizing I have a choice is so liberating. I've decided to start acting like I do. I can even choose what kind of work I do, whether I work part-time or full-time. I choose to work part-time for someone else and a paycheck—and then use the rest of the weekdays for writing, exercising and solitude.

It was Oprah who reminded me that I have a choice and that joy is our birthright. Joy. For many, that's a novel idea. Most people don't even expect to experience real joy in their lives. Instead, they just hope to get along. But when we decide to live a joyous life, boy what a decision that is.

Again I've picked up Julia Cameron's The Artist's Way. *I felt I could use this writer's gentle words of encouragement right now as I make this transition from well-paying drudgery to what I love. The paragraph that I must record here speaks directly to me. Cameron writes:* "What we really want to do is what we are really meant to do. When we do what we are meant to do, money come to us, doors open for us, we feel useful, and the work we do feels like play to us." *That's it. Oprah is known to say,* "Do what you love, the money will come." *She also operates from her instincts. Well, this is what I'm going after.*

It appears I took the long way by first going to law school, but I know I had to do that before I could do anything else. I'm so clear about this. I'm glad I got a law degree still. I am meant to do work that makes me feel useful. Right now, this job makes me feel useless. I've tried, but haven't been able to find my niche. I am clear that God doesn't support waste. I'm wasting myself here. It's interesting how so many people waste themselves while trying desperately to convince themselves and others that it is okay—even justified—so they can pay the bills. If we really trust God, we would know God wants us to do His will—and to pay our bills.

When I told my friend Denene of my plans to leave, she looked at me like one of my eyeballs hung from its socket. Undaunted, I continued to excitedly tell her of my plans. Then she got it. Initially, however, she tried to tell me I should do what lots of people in state government do—do what they love while they pretend to do the state's work. No. No. I am ready to fully live the life I really want, instead of the one I thought I wanted.

I just had a revelatory thought, maybe this path I'm on is simply a natural progression toward liberation, I mean moving from being a lawyer to just a successful person. Successful because I know who I am, not because of the title I hold. There's hope. I've seen a change in me with respect to this "I am a lawyer" fixation. I really,

really desired to be a lawyer, but I never thought about how that would help me to serve others. I just desperately wanted to feel like somebody. I wanted to be one of the "important" people in this society. I wanted to feel powerful, to feel as good as I thought "the good people" felt. I am so glad I was able to go to law school, to sit for and pass the bar, to practice worker's compensation law for two and a half years. I grew tremendously from these experiences.

But in the process of becoming a lawyer, I also discovered how little I wanted to actually practice law. Nonetheless, I loved being a lawyer, that is, I loved the prestige it brought me. Now I'm getting to a place where I no longer need to wear my degree on my sleeve. I feel like somebody whether others know I'm a lawyer or not. Hallelujah!

A GRANDER VISION OF YOURSELF

There is a direct link between addictions and not living our purpose. Living a passionate, purposeful life feeds our spirit, brings us unspeakable joy, and thereby reduces our yen for destructive substances and behaviors. We pine for the enchanted life. Our souls hunger for a reason to bound from bed in the morning and venture into the world. As long as we settle for work, love and/or a lifestyle that betrays the highest vision we hold for our lives— or the one God ordained for us—we are vulnerable to acting out addictively. We aren't meant to hate our life. And we don't have to hate it. We have the power of choice. We can consciously choose a life we can love. Sure, it takes courage. You're find that inside you.

Hold a grander vision of yourself. Everyday do something, no matter how small, that helps to bring that vision into manifestation. We have the power. It lies in the daily choices that we make. Believe in you, and let that belief decide for you.

37

AT LAST

I don't want my life to obey any other will but my own.

SIMONE DE BEAUVOIR, *The Second Sex*

There is an applause superior to that of the multitude—one's own.

ELIZABETH ELTON SMITH

FOR SO MANY YEARS, THE SHADOW BELIEF—THAT I WAS damaged, unlovable and undeserving—drove me to repeat the same self-destructive behaviors over and over again. Yet every new relationship, job and experience pushed me closer to becoming the woman I am today—a resilient woman of strength, character, and integrity.

I continue to work against the tendency toward self-devaluation and conditional self-acceptance. Nonetheless, thank God, I am much further along the path that leads to a sense of wholeness and unconditional love than I once thought possible.

Several months ago, I gradually grew increasingly disillusioned with the spiritual detour that I'd taken two years earlier. I'd resumed attending the orthodox Christian church, after years of disenchantment with organized religion. But when confusion and a sense of powerlessness consumed me, I knew I had to make a change. My heart and soul set out on a quiet but determined quest to find a more suitable spiritual path—one that would strengthen, empower and give me more clarity at the end of the day.

I'd also given myself a long overdue gift—I entered individual therapy.

One Wednesday evening as I collapsed onto the sofa across from my therapist Rosie, inhaling, I casually offered, "*This is the one place where I can stop, and have nothing asked of me.*" She knowingly looked at me with those smiling eyes. The following week, at the end of our session, she introduced me to the Labyrinth, showing me a postcard picture of it. She proffered it as a space where I might slow down, gather myself, and find my way back inward. Then she handed me a list of seven Labyrinths in the Maryland area.

The Labyrinth is a spiritual tool that has been around for thousands of years as a symbolic path to the Holy Land, one that leads us to the heart of God. It is not a maze. The way in also leads out.

Early Thursday morning, I walked my first Labyrinth on the grounds of the St. Anthony of Padua Church. Not coincidentally, it was located only minutes away from the bus stop where I'd drive my daughter Adia every morning to catch a yellow bus to McDonogh's summer camp. Walking the Labyrinth was an emotionally charged and spiritually liberating experience. As Rosie promised, it helped to turn my attention inwards, where the answers to my most pressing problems could be found.

A WORK IN PROGRESS

On another occasion, I spent five hours at the Santa Rosa Labyrinth located in Northeast Baltimore on the grounds of Govans Presbyterian Church. It was incredibly calming to sit on the wood bench beneath the canopy of magnificent trees. Across from the bench was erected a statue of two biblical male figures, one kneeling seemingly pleading with the taller one—presumably Jesus—for healing or mercy. I alternately journaled and read *Awakening the Buddha Within: Eight Steps to Enlightenment.*

Then I walked the dirt and graveled Labyrinth barefooted because I wanted the experience to attempt to simulate life's oftentimes uneven, thorny terrain. The walk, as expected, was prickly and rough. It was a simple yet strangely profound reminder that one's capacity to persist through difficulty is limitless as long as one believes intensely that the path she's on leads her home to God.

At the end of the day, as I power walked through Druid Hill Park, I reflected on my day. I'd spent an entire day alone, in solitude and silence, communing with Spirit. Not once did I feel alone or lonely. Not once did I think, "*If only I had a man in my life I would...*" Sure, like any healthy heterosexual woman, I desire to share my life with a loving man. I, however, am no longer held hostage by the illusion that a man can cure any of life's challenges. At last, I am quite clear that no man—irrespective of his character, stature or wealth—will define, complete or validate me. No, that is my job. One I am now happy to assume fully. To be sure, it is work that continues. As I remain a work in progress. As do you.